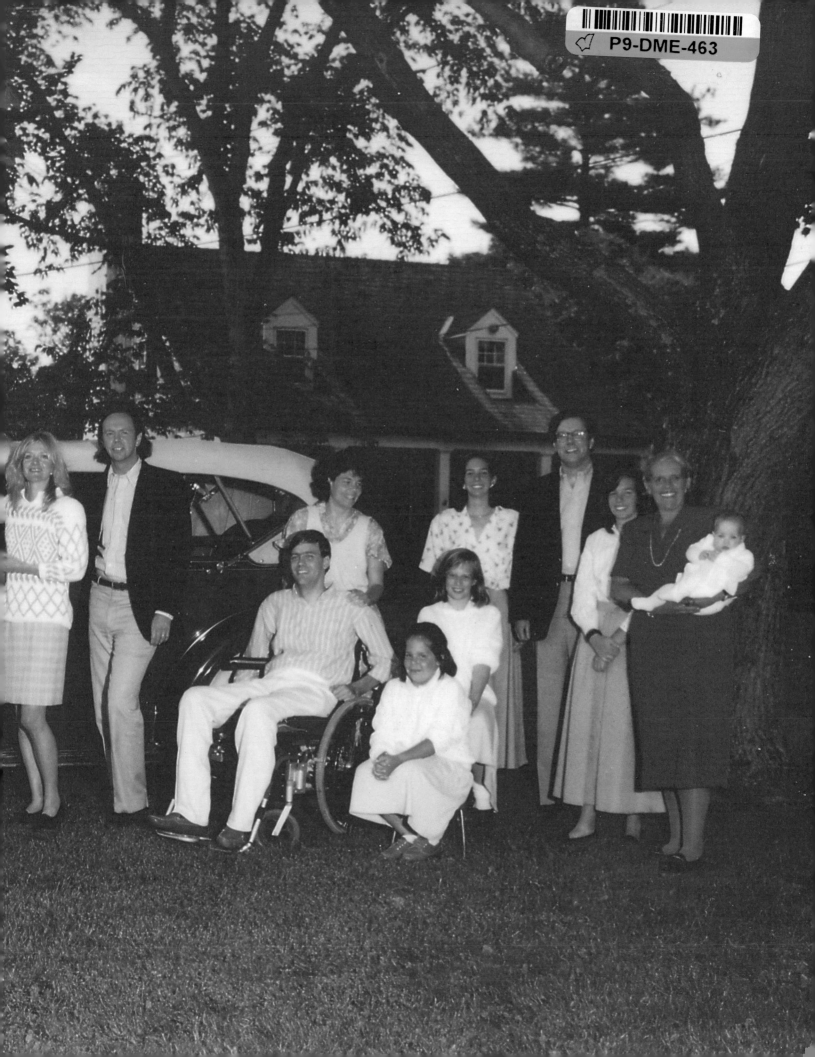

By Malcolm Forbes

MORE THAN I DREAMED

THEY WENT THAT-A-WAY . . .
(with Jeff Bloch)

THE FURTHER SAYINGS OF CHAIRMAN MALCOLM

AROUND THE WORLD ON HOT AIR AND TWO WHEELS

THE SAYINGS OF CHAIRMAN MALCOLM

FACT AND COMMENT

THE FORBES SCRAPBOOK OF THOUGHTS ON THE BUSINESS OF LIFE

MORE THAN I DREAMED

by

Malcolm Forbes

EDITED BY TONY CLARK

SIMON AND SCHUSTER

NEW YORK · LONDON · TORONTO · SYDNEY · TOKYO

SIMON AND SCHUSTER
SIMON & SCHUSTER BUILDING
ROCKEFELLER CENTER
1230 AVENUE OF THE AMERICAS
NEW YORK, NEW YORK 10020

COPYRIGHT © 1989 BY MALCOLM FORBES

DESIGNED BY EVE METZ
MANUFACTURED IN SPAIN

1   3   5   7   9   10   8   6   4   2

LIBRARY OF CONGRESS CATALOGING IN PUBLICATION DATA
FORBES, MALCOLM S.
MORE THAN I DREAMED/BY MALCOLM FORBES; EDITED BY TONY CLARK.
P.   CM.
1. FORBES, MALCOLM S.   2. BUSINESSMEN—UNITED STATES—
BIOGRAPHY.   3. CAPITALISTS AND FINANCIERS—UNITED STATES—
BIOGRAPHY.   4. MILLIONAIRES—UNITED STATES—BIOGRAPHY.   I. CLARK, TONY.
II. TITLE.
HC102.5.F67A3   1989
338.7′61070572′0924—DC19   89-4305
[B]   CIP
ISBN 0-671-67121-9

PREVIOUS PAGE: *L-R: Timothy C. Forbes, Malcolm S. Forbes, Jr., Christopher Forbes, MF, Robert L. Forbes; "Fathers and Sons in America," photograph by Dennis Manarchy, October 21, 1987.*

To son Christopher
whose friendship, love, genius and wit
have been instrumental
in making this life
"More Than I Dreamed"

I never cease to be amazed at how much work by many people is involved in putting together a book like this. In-house, without the endless hours of input by photography-knowledgeable son Bob, the job still wouldn't be done. Because he was a key player in much that follows, his editorial assistance has been invaluable.

Without that appealing, tireless, cheerful resource, Forbes' archivist, Tammy Rodgers, we wouldn't have been able to put our hands on most of what's depicted. Though it has required a whopping amount of hours, for the three of us this project has been fun.

Simon and Schuster's brilliant Eve Metz, who put together the earlier companion volume to this one—*Around the World on Hot Air and Two Wheels*—has done it again.

If you like what you see, thank them.

If you don't . . .

As for the author, it may be my life, but this book involves a lot of their work.

MALCOLM FORBES

CONTENTS

FOREWARNED
page 13

CHAPTER ONE
MORE THAN I DREAMED
page 20

CHAPTER TWO
MESSING ABOUT IN BOATS
page 48

CHAPTER THREE
THE HIGHWAYMAN
page 96

CHAPTER FOUR
ABOVE AND BEYOND
page 118

CHAPTER FIVE
NO PLACES LIKE HOME
page 168

CHAPTER SIX
GETTING IT ALL TOGETHER
page 204

CHAPTER SEVEN
R.S.V.P.
page 224

Forewarned

Every once in a while a writer in dearth will write me a letter saying they're thinking about doing a book about me.

I write back and say how flattering the thought is. The idea that someone thinks enough people might be interested in a book about you is certainly ego adrenaline. But I go on to explain that for quite a while I've been putting into a file stuff for an autobiography. So, being of mostly Scottish blood from a father all so and a mother partly so, I feel a proprietary interest in the subject and would appreciate if they left my life story to me.

This book is part of that tale. *More Than I Dreamed* deals with the genesis of the accoutrements that have accumulated during the life of a collector who never set out to be one.

I guess what's happened is that when certain things turn you on and you accumulate enough of them, voila! It's a collection and you're a collector.

But what you see in the first half dozen pages of pictures here is *the* collection, the one that fulfills beyond measure, is unduplicatable and of a value incalculable. Since Bertie and I said our I Do's 43 years ago, twenty-one of us now sit down at the family table on Thanksgiving, Christmas, Easter and often for no reason at all except wanting to have the fun we have just being together.

One thing this volume does is to eliminate the need for illustrations in the more ruminative autobiography I'm now marinating.

Putting this together has been a ball, and I hope you'll enjoy waltzing through it.

MF

The Forbes quintette Bruce, Duncan, Malcolm, Gordon Wallace and their composers are thinking of you lovingly. You are always as welcome at our home as Santa Claus.

1928

1946

1947

1949

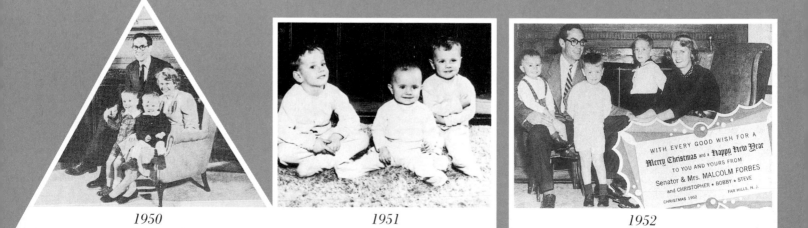

1950

1951

1952

1953

1954

1955

1956

1958

1959

1960

1961

1962

1963

1964

1965

1966

1967

1968

1969

1970

16 • MORE THAN I DREAMED

1971

1972

1973

1974

1975

1976

1977

1978

1979

1980

1981

1982

1983

1984

1985

1986

1987

1988

CHAPTER

1

MORE
THAN I
DREAMED

LIVING AND DREAMING
are two different things—but you can't
do one without the other.

From The Sayings of Chairman Malcolm

T HE DREAMS OF CHILDHOOD are so circum-
scribed by circumstances they have little or no
impact on life as it unfolds, except one: they
are fun to recollect. Who has failed to chuckle
over memories of early
desires? The excitement
of being a fireman. The
importance of being a
policeman. The drama of
being the coalman re-
sponsible for sending
those black lumps thun-
dering from the truck
down the metal sluice to
the furnace room. I had
a Buddy-L bus, and as I
steered it from room to
room, how my mind ro-
manced about driving a
real one all over Amer-
ica. The ultimate glory of
being the man who
leaned out the window of
the steam locomotive, in
charge of getting that
great trainload of people
to where they were going
and on time.

Often equally chimeri-
cal are teen dreams. Turned onto flying by
Lindbergh's wondrous solo flight across the
great Atlantic to Paris. The excitement of Election Day. One day maybe to be mayor. Or governor. Or senator. Or President? Someday to
be the Boss, to own the place where we sum-
mer-job. If it's in business or the professions or
whatever, to be the best, to be at the top.

And, of course, to make and have money.
Lots of it.

These pages are not very much about young
dreams realized, but really about a life of happenings and possessions I never remotely
dreamed of. Almost all of them are byproducts

of total encompassing enthusiasm doing the job
my father did before me.

So we begin with memories of him.

These memories are at flood tide because recently B. C. Forbes' two still-living sons and
some of his grandchildren and great-grandchil-
dren returned from Scotland, where we re-
buried him in the plot of his grandparents by
the kirk that had such a lasting impact on
him throughout his seventy-four years of life.

*The first cover: In September 1917, $1,000
was a lot of money.*

But more of that later.
My parents, Bertie
Forbes and Adelaide
Stevenson, were married
in New York in 1915. My
oldest brother, Bruce,
was born about a year
after they were wed,
and a year and a half
later Duncan, a second
brother, was born. I was
the third, showing up in
Brooklyn on August 19,
1919. Five years later appeared brother number
four, Gordon, who died
in 1988. Nine years later
came Wallace, who cel-
ebrated his sixtieth
birthday last year.

Now Wally and I are
the only surviving broth-
ers of the five. I was so
close in age to Duncan
and Bruce we had the
usual sibling rivalries. We often did battle. We
were all quite different in capabilities, attitudes
and appetites. With the two younger brothers,
Gordon and Wally, there was a sufficient age
gap so they were not considered either contemporaries or competitors, but rather kid brothers
to be counseled or patronized.

My memories of growing up, while not rose-
colored, are basically happy ones. But I think
growing up is the most difficult thing in the
world to do. The painting of childhood—anyone's—as idyllic is nonsense.

The first word infants learn is not "Dada" or
"Mama." It's "No-no." "No" this. "No" that.

PREVIOUS SPREAD: *Pitsligo Castle, built by Sir William Forbes in the
early 15th century. We purchased the ruin on June 18, 1988, from Mr.
George Chalmers, whose family had farmed there since 1913.*

B. C. Forbes and siblings circa 1900, five brothers and four sisters. Back row (L–R): Willie, Alex, Gina, Wilson, Aggie, Jim, Anna; Front row (L–R): Tibbie, Robert (B.C.'s father), Duncan, Agnes Moir (B.C.'s mother), B.C.

"I do" to Adelaide Stevenson, April 20, 1915.

B. C. Forbes at age 37 in 1917, the year Forbes was founded. Dad was a past president of the Burns Society.

The Roaring '20s, cloche hats and a fedora. Aboard the President Hayes in Boston Harbor, September 6, 1927.

Dad proudly at the wheel of his first car— a Model T, circa 1913.

MORE THAN I DREAMED • 23

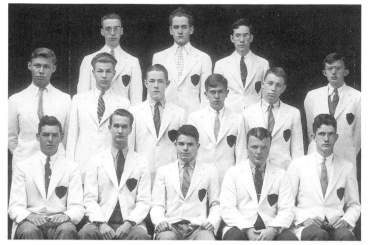

Cum Laude Society, Lawrenceville, 1937. MF in top row, right end.

"No" to everything we do when we begin to be able to do anything. It continues right up to "Can we go to the movies?" and "Can I borrow the car?" It's nos and warnings and admonishments and questions of where, why, who and what until we're out of house and larder.

Growing up properly or improperly, well or badly, is anything but easy. Every day, every year, something or many things are new. There's the pressure of contemporaries from playground to kindergarten and right through school. Whether you are good at a sport or not. Whether you are able to have a bike or take a hike. Whether you can get permission to do what your buddies are planning to do.

When you are young, you swing from crisis to crisis. There is no sense of perspective. No sense of time and its length. You have a fight with someone, or your girlfriend won't talk to you when you're nine or ten years old, and you think this is forever. Everything is monumental —it seems *years* between birthdays, *years* be-

tween Christmases, *years* between when you're fourteen and know how to drive to when you can have your own license.

It's only when we're grown-up that time telescopes.

I don't think earning a living is half as difficult as going to school, doing homework and getting through college. By the time you've survived growing up and educating your parents on how to raise children, just going out and earning a living is a comparative breeze, the freedom exhilarating.

I guess writing and publishing and having opinions about everything have been in my blood from the beginning. My mother and father bought a house on Fountain Road in Englewood, New Jersey, before their firstborn was. And it was there that, at a very early age, I started my first newspaper, *The City of Dunc News*. It reported the happenings of a cardboard city that Gordon and I constructed in the basement. The town had a population of 250 lead people, about sixty Tootsie Toy automobiles and several shoebox factories. Every evening we two became part of that little town, living out its activities and problems and then hunt-and-peck-typing out our imagined news of the day in the *City of Dunc*, sold to anyone in our house, or anyone who ventured near.

Maybe we were improperly raised, because one of my less happy childhood recollections is the first Christmas that my "big" present was a suit. I'd have filed a suit if we'd had lawyers then as we have now. Parents were *supposed* to clothe you, and to clothe you in the guise of

Camp Kawanhee, 1929. MF is 18th from the left, first row.

24 • MORE THAN I DREAMED

RIGHT: *The dog was Mickey Finn. Others (clockwise from lower left): Duncan, Gordon, B.C., Bruce, Malcolm, Adelaide, and Wally.*

The last copy of MF's first newspaper.

Circa 1929. MF is the one on top.

An early-on editorial exhortation: Fire Prevention essay and medal, 6th grade.

Christmas presents didn't smack of fraud, it *was* fraud. I think only in that regard were we in any real sense "spoiled" kids.

My most memorable Christmas present was received in 1931. I was probably the only twelve-year-old in America yearning for a mimeograph machine. Since the age of seven, I'd been turning out "newspapers" for home and neighborhood, reproducing them on a tin of gelatin which would absorb a special purple typewriter ink that enabled you to make a dozen or so copies by pressing a special paper on top of the transfer.

Mimeographing—a word now virtually Xeroxed into extinction—was the foremost way of making inexpensive copies. The A. B. Dick Company's smallest one ($35) included a box of stencils, some lettering guides and some styluses. It was the depth of the Depression, and I doubted that my father, then struggling to keep *Forbes* magazine alive, could afford to make my great wish come true by stuffing one into Santa's Forbes family bag.

The following article on Fire Prevention was written by Malcolm Forbes. It won the first prize in a contest given throughout the Englewood schools.

FIRE PREVENTION

Hark! The fire whistle! Who was careless? Was it a man or a child?

The cause of so many fires is our carelessness. If we would obey the rules made by people who have had experience there would be fewer fires.

You and I have seen many picnicers. They thoughtlessly leave papers and refuse wherever they had eaten. Some of the men smoked and threw the unsmoked remnants on the ground. This has often started fires which have spread rapidly through dried leaves. Many of these fires have made great headways before noticed and began the much feared forest fires. All because someone was

indifferent to the rules for fire prevention. They could not fail to see the printed warning posted everywhere along the highways pleading for care.

Not only picnicers are careless but each day newspapers carry reports of horrible fires and deaths because housewives are not careful. Rubbish of one kind or another is piled up. Some day they plan to clean it away but often delay means disaster, for that very pile of useless refuse catches fire and the house and sometimes lives are lost.

Electric appliances such as ironers, curling irons, etc. Are left on, and in a short time another tragedy is in the newspaper.

Let us then do our part to help others be careful by being careful ourselves for after all "Example is better than Recipe."

He did, and almost overnight my publishing career ignited. Two weeks later was born an eight-page Scout *Eagle* for the Boy Scout troop of which I (and, incidentally, in those same years the future Secretary of State, George Schultz) was a member; then the *Hackley Eagle*, which I published during my first year away at prep school in competition with the weekly school paper.

From Hackley, the mimeograph and I went to Lawrenceville, where students were domiciled in eight separate houses. Within days the *Kennedy House Eagle* was in full flourish, and my journalistic outpourings extended so far into the night that at the request of roommates I wrote home pleading for a noiseless typewriter.

At Princeton, I failed in the competition to get on the *Daily Princetonian*, and at the beginning of sophomore year, I dragooned some classmates into helping launch *The Nassau Sovereign*. It aimed to supersede the purely literary magazine and bring to the college campus the *Time/Life* sort of journalism that was then sweeping the country. The *Sovereign* survived a decade, with time out for World War II.

Princeton Gymnastics Team, 1940. It's the only college letter I was good enough to win. My specialty was the rope climb, a skill that led to a meteoric rise in the infantry, helping me attain the rank of Acting Corporal and, more important, exempting me from KP.

Princeton Class Medal, 1941, awarded to the student "who has done the most for PRINCETON and his Class."

Lawrenceville medals, 1937. (L–R): The Lit, The Bibliophiles, *Pipe & Quill,* Olla Podrida, *and Cum Laude. Was I glad in those days that we had pocket watches and chains.*

Trying to look as if MF was saving the country single-handedly. Camp Howze, Texas, 1942.

The prime responsibility of a Princeton undergraduate's final year is the senior thesis. I wrote mine about U.S. weekly newspapers. My "great plan" on graduating was eventually to build a chain of weeklies in a politically consequential state where agriculture and industry were in reasonable balance—which turned out to be Ohio. In those days, weeklies flourished in areas predominantly rural. I figured that with a large number of them I could matter politically while enjoying the pleasure of columnizing

and editorializing à la William Allen White.

And I didn't want to work for my father at *Forbes*. I feared friction, because Dad certainly ran his business, and I figured it would be far more fun to be able to run my own.

So on graduating I spent a quick couple of weeks checking out weeklies that were for sale in the Buckeye State and borrowed the money from my father's friends—I was afraid to ask him—to acquire *The Fairfield Times*, printed in a back alley in Lancaster, Ohio. It was a rough learning experience. With five on the payroll, I spent much time selling ads and on Thursdays, when the paper appeared, running around to collect for them so that I could meet Friday's payroll.

Five months later Pearl Harbor was attacked, and a while after that I was a private in the Infantry. On a salary of $90 a month, it proved impossible to meet the $125 weekly salary of the editor who had been hired to carry on, and I used a ten-day leave to close up the operation for the duration. With newsprint extremely scarce and strictly rationed, I was able to arrange with our competitor, in return for our newsprint quota, to keep the paper's name alive in a supplement they were printing for the area's men in service.

Ours was the first trainload of inductees that chugged into Camp Howze, Texas, to begin fleshing out the 84th Railsplitter Division's skeleton cadre. Assigned to the heavy-machine-gun section in Company D of the 334th Regiment, I gradually made it up the ladder to staff sergeant. Our division eventually arrived in England, and many weeks after D-Day we landed

Four war medals (top): Combat Infantry Badge; (bottom L-R): Bronze Star, Purple Heart, Good Conduct.

Three and a half years was enough.

Sharp Shooter medal (left): Rifle, Carbine, Pistol, Machine Gun. Dog Tags: With you until the end.

The Presidential Citizens Medal: Awarded to MF by President Reagan, January 18, 1989.

MF's Miniature Medals (L-R): Bronze Star, Purple Heart, Presidential Citizens, Good Conduct, American Campaign, European Theater, Order of St. John, Legion of Honor, Order of Merit of the Republique Francaise, Commander of the Order of Arts and Letters, Moroccan Commander of the Order of Ouissam Alaouite, The Most Honorable Order of the Crown of Thailand, The Pakistani President's Medal of Achievement.

Roberta Laidlaw Forbes—a stunning, shy, sweet, blue-eyed blond.

Wedding day, September 21, 1946. Back row (L–R): Jim Millikin, Gordon Forbes, Wally Forbes, MF, Gil Dunklin, Lou Pyle, Bob Campbell, Ned Chase (father of Chevy). Front row (L–R): Jack Barker, Richard Stickel, Henry Peters, Bruce Forbes, John Kearns.

on the Normandy beachhead and were trucked to Montgomery's Ninth Army, where we were assigned a sector near Amiens.

A few days before the German breakthrough in the Battle of the Bulge, I was hit by a German patrol while trying to locate the outfit that was supposed to be anchoring our positions. For discovering there was no one at the link-up point, in addition to the Purple Heart I was awarded the Bronze Star for preventing the "possible encirclement of the battalion," and I spent the next nine months in the hospital while a shattered left thigh bone mended.

In the final stages of regaining the limb's use, I devoted a lot of time to studying *Forbes* magazine, its content and its layout. On a visit home

I expressed a bushel-basketful of ideas to my father, and he suggested that on discharge I come to work. His offer of $100 a week contrasted wonderfully with my GI income. Acceptance was quick and enthusiastic.

As was (almost) my love-at-first-sight proposal to Bertie Laidlaw, a stunning, shy, sweet blue-eyed Veronica Lake–tressed blond nineteen-year-old. My brothers and I had known her older sisters before the war. We met during my last weekend in the Army, and, though still on crutches, I made the most of my sharply pressed tan uniform, Railsplitter patch, sergeant's stripes, Combat Infantry badge and ribbons. It was at a cocktail party of Englewood's young, celebrating the about-to-be-announced

Dad dances at our wedding.

Aboard the Swedish American liner Stockholm, *which later sank the* Andrea Doria; *circa 1950.*

Home from the honeymoon. This time, the dog was Rondyke.

That campaign essential, the "Family Togetherness" photo: the Candidate, with (L–R):Robert (Bob), Malcolm, Jr. (Steve), Christopher (Kip), and Bertie, 1952.

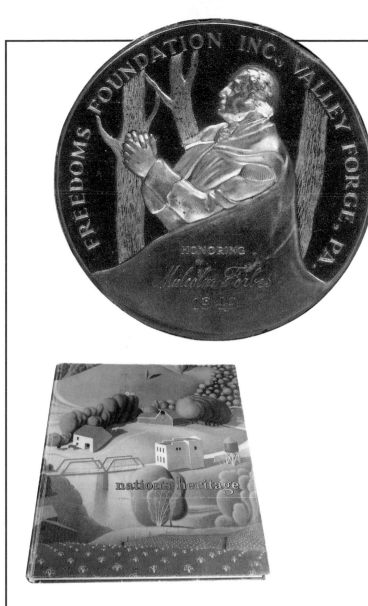

ORTY YEARS AGO I received an A for a pioneering publishing effort but an F for the bottom-line results. For two years I'd been consumed by the vision of a book-bound, extra-large, advertisingless six-times-a-year magazine that would be principally illustrative, to picture the heritage belonging to all Americans in a manner that would have the greatest appeal to most Americans.

We launched the first issue of *Nation's Heritage* with an elaborate all-day reception in the Empire Room of the Waldorf-Astoria Hotel. It received a decent degree of critical acclaim. But I had put so much of what we could spare in those far leaner years into the magazine itself, there was little left to promote and sell it.

Before the year was out, it was obvious that we were not going to garner enough $150 subscriptions to make an appreciable dent in our considerable publishing costs. A byproduct of those youthful dreamer days often is an enthusiastic conviction blinding one to tough sharp-pencil cost calculations.

While red ink marked the failure, a gold medal was awarded for good intentions. At historic Valley Forge, General Dwight D. Eisenhower—then president of Columbia University —on behalf of the Freedoms Foundation awarded me their gold medal inscribed: "Malcolm S. Forbes, publisher of *Nation's Heritage*, for outstanding achievement in bringing about a better understanding of the American Way of Life."

Running for Governor on 400 New Jersey bill-boards.

Photo-op, Gubernatorial campaign, 1957. Saddled up (L–R): Kip, Steve and Bob with Bertie.

Japanese surrender. Literally, I ended up my enthusiastic conversation with her by declaring with ardent sincerity that I hoped she would marry me.

We were not formally engaged until that winter, and just about a year later, on September 21, 1946, we did it. At our wedding Dad, for the first time in years, put on his kilt and danced. Through Bertie's Laidlaw veins ran a fair amount of Scottish blood, too.

In the fifties, while parenting four sons, Malcolm Jr. (Steve), Bob, Christopher (Kip) and Tim, and a daughter, Moira, I served a term as Bernardsville, N.J., Borough Councilman and in 1951 ran for the New Jersey State Senate in Somerset County, which had become our home. I rang eighteen thousand doorbells, was bitten by thirteen dogs and won with the largest margin ever recorded. In 1953 I competed unsuccessfully for the Republican gubernatorial nomination against the Republican organization's choice, who blew it in November.

Four years later I was the GOP gubernatorial nominee, to oppose Democratic incumbent Robert Meyner, at whom, unfortunately, no-

THIS THIRTY-TWO-YEAR-OLD PHOTOGRAPH is a delightful reminder of the poignant phoniness of so much political campaigning—expensively engineered synthetic hoopla and crafted enthusiasm.

Here my wife and I are, in a horn-tooting motorcade, proceeding down the main street of Hackensack, New Jersey, a month before the November 1957 gubernatorial election when I was the Republican candidate for governor.

If you look carefully, you won't find a voter on the sidewalks; my waving glad hand is aimed at what must have been the only soul in sight— the photographer. Note the unenthusiastic expression of the be-orchided Bergen County lady leader. Each car and driver in the motorcade cost our campaign twenty-five bucks plus free drinks and feed at the subsequent arduously gathered "mass rally."

Yet would you believe that on the eve of being nosed out by a record landslide, I thought we'd win?

For politicos, 'tis easy to succumb to self-deception.

Vice-President Nixon gives MF's campaign a hand; Atlantic City, 1957

body was mad. As the campaign wore on, it became apparent that about the only major issue was my wanting the job he had. It didn't help when he pointed out in the Camden shipyards, where wartime-flush employment was sharply withering, that I was building our first *Highlander* yacht in the Netherlands.

It didn't help, either, when he outsmarted us with a most clever trick. We had announced that we were beginning the first-ever twenty-four-hour campaign telethon on New Jersey's only TV channel (which later became PBS's Channel 13). Governor Meyner strategically booked the thirty minutes before our starting time. After a twenty-minute speech by the Governor, they played the National Anthem for ten minutes, so everybody assumed the station was going off the air, or they put it off their air.

In retrospect, perhaps, losing that election was lucky. Vice-President Nixon campaigned for me, and we developed a good rapport. Had I become governor, in all probability I would have gone to Washington when he later became President, and by now perhaps would have been in jail, have written a book about it and be lecturing to ever-dwindling audiences.

My father had died in 1954, and running our business was requiring more and more of my time, with not enough left over to continue being really effective in politics. My oldest brother, Bruce, and I had inherited one third each of the shares of Forbes Inc., with one sixth going to each of our two younger brothers, who were not active in the company. After Dad's death I became editor and publisher, and Bruce president. When Bruce died, in 1964, we re-

tired his shares at the request of his widow. Sometime later, we did the same with Gordon's one sixth and Wally's, so that I was the sole stockholder. Our annual stockholder's meeting tended to be brief. In recent years my children have become minority stockholders, but the annual meeting continues to be brief.

Often when on university campuses to address graduating classes, I am asked how one becomes successful, and I explain that my own success was attributable to sheer ability—spelled i-n-h-e-r-i-t-a-n-c-e. "If you can pick a parent who owns a business and be sure he's not mad at you when he checks out, it's a surer way to the top than anything else that comes to mind."

Almost seventy-four years before Dad passed on and passed on to us Forbes Inc., he was born (1880) in most modest circumstances in the parish of Whitehill, New Deer, Aberdeenshire, the sixth of ten children. His father was a country storekeeper and did some tailoring. His grandfather a blacksmith. He left school to become an apprentice printer's devil, and at twenty-one left Scotland for South Africa to become a reporter and an assistant to columnist Edgar Wallace at the founding of the *Rand Daily Mail* in Johannesburg. Saving every cent possible, he came to America in 1904 and got his first job by offering to work for nothing as a reporter for the *Journal of Commerce*. A dozen years later he had become a widely syndicated business columnist. In 1917, as an outlet for his outpourings that were too voluminous for his daily column and his other magazine feature articles, he founded *Forbes*.

New Deer, Aberdeenshire—the house where my father was born and grew up.

My memories of Dad during my growing-up years are very strong, very powerful. He was an emphatic man, older than most fathers, because he hadn't married until he was thirty-five. He could be stern, but was not overly so. Obedience was absolutely at the top of his list.

He was also very insistent about schoolwork. When you got home you did your chores, inside or out in the garden, depending on the time of year. The first thing he would ask when he got home at night around seven o'clock was, "Have you done your homework?"

In those days, parents had to sign your monthly report card, and that was always a fearful day, the degree of fearsomeness depending on how many marks you had below B. A's were rewarded both verbally and with a little coin of the realm. C's were a cause for considerable comment—"Why? What is the difficulty?"—and a D created consternation, for that was failure.

The counter to this sort of thing was the family fun we had together. We'd pile into the car with Dad on a Saturday and go to Palisades Amusement Park, which stood for years above the Hudson just north of Fort Lee, New Jersey. Another junket highlight was a ride down to the penny candy store to gleefully agonize over the spending of a windfall quarter.

I vividly remember Christmas in 1928, when my father presented to the family our first movie camera. The latest thing then, it was several times bulkier than those available today, and it was fed fifty-foot 16mm black-and-white film. It was considerably more complicated to operate, and the results were quite a bit below what amateurs can achieve with today's equipment.

The thing that most sticks in my mind is the constant admonition from Dad when the camera was in use: "Move! This is moving pictures!" Being a good Scotsman, he felt that standing still in front of a motion picture camera was a waste. The result was, of course, such constant hustle, bustle and scurrying in our early home movies that one could seldom tell who was who or what, or who looked how, or even what the occasion was and where.

Some summers ago when my own family clan toured Europe, we repeated the same error after the acquisition of a zoom lens. Everybody who took a turn at recording some eminently perishable scene had to zoom in and out—after all, wasn't that what a zoom lens was for? The result is some of the most dizzying home movies ever made.

Mother and Dad also enjoyed occasions that gave us joy, and birthday parties were very important. Duncan's birthday was August 25 and mine August 19. They were close together, but we never had a joint party. Each one was always made to feel that his birthday was *his* day. These were the kinds of indulgences that my parents put great stock in.

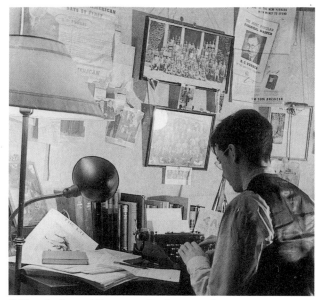

Like father, like son. B.C. punching out the first copy of Forbes, *1917; MF and the noiseless typewriter, Lawrenceville, 1937.*

In 1930, to mark his fiftieth year, my father gave each of his five sons a $1,000 Cities Service bond. As a ten-year-old with a ten-cent allowance (a dime went pretty far in a five-and-dime store in those days), I found it hard to conceptualize this enormous gift. But Lesson One came rapidly.

I'd been yearning, pleading, saving for and nagging, cajoling, dreaming about a balloon-tired, chrome-fendered bicycle that our local Sears, Roebuck store had on display. It cost $38.50. When Dad, with befitting solemnity, handed each of us his bond, my joy was unbounded. Using $38.50 from it would be a relatively insignificant withdrawal to buy my bike.

But when I excitedly turned to Mother and asked how soon we could get to Sears, Father thundered, "Bonds are not for cashing in. They are security for the future."

No bike.

At the time of the gift, I thought with bitter disappointment how much I'd rather have had the bike than the bond. It turned out I'd have had more if I had had the bike instead of the bond. Three years later—1933—the bond itself was virtually worthless.

Another thing about my father: every morning he would read the Bible. We would go in to

Mr. Hearst's New York American *promotes B.C.'s syndicated daily column, which appeared in almost 100 newspapers.*

see him early on a Saturday or a Sunday (because on schooldays we were gone long before he was), and after he had dressed and was get-

*B.C.'s New Deer
Reunion Picnics.*

ting ready to go downstairs he would always open the Bible on his bureau there and read a verse or two and say his prayers to himself.

And then every night, like brushing your teeth, you had to say your prayers before you got into bed. No matter if you just knelt down and pretended and your mind was on something else, you at least had to go through the motions.

Also, almost every Sunday we had to learn a hymn. We were paid a dime when we could recite the words, and we couldn't go out to play until we did. I don't remember any of the hymns very fully now, but they come roaring back at a church service when you open the book and voices ring out.

How my father loved to play poker. He played every Sunday, with five or six family friends and others, a game that was interrupted only to hear us with our hymn-of-the-week. As we got older, it struck us as incongruous—interrupting a Sabbath poker game to sound off hymnally. But it was a sacred Sunday ritual.

I remember my father as hard-working, principled. He was a great believer in sensible frugality—a true Scot. He was a firm father but understanding, with a high degree of tolerance, so long as we didn't violate his fundamental dictums.

Mother, very much her own woman, was quite different. Before the term was invented, Mother was a practicing Keynesian. A nice Catholic girl from Brooklyn. One of their most memorable set-tos occurred when she put a lot of checks before him in the depths of the

ANOTHER MILESTONE

Ed Marcus, editorial cartoonist for The New York Times, *was a longtime friend of B.C. and a favorite checker game opponent. Periodically, he drew apropos cartoons for* Forbes *as well.*

WITH THE GREATEST OF EASE

Luncheon "21"
May 28, 1951.

Wining and dining a top tableful of "America's 8 Leading Businessmen":
Forbes *luncheon, "21" Club, May 28, 1951. B.C. furnished the beef-and-kidney pie. Seated (L–R): Dr. Allen B. DuMont, Founder, DuMont Television Network; John L. Collyer, President, B.F. Goodrich; Eddie Rickenbacker, President, Eastern Airlines; New Jersey Governor Alfred E. Driscoll; Thomas J. Watson, Chairman, IBM: A. P. Sloan, Jr., Chairman, General Motors; Standing (L–R): B. C. Forbes; Robert R. Young, Chairman, C&O Railroad; MF; Benjamin F. Fairless, President, U.S. Steel; Harvey S. Firestone, Jr., Chairman, Firestone Tire & Rubber; and Bruce Forbes.*

M.V. "Brittanic"
August 19, 1948

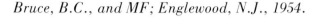
B.C. aboard the Brittanic, *August 1948, en route to Scotland.*

Bruce, B.C., and MF; Englewood, N.J., 1954.

Depression. He bellowed, "How can you spend so much money?" "Bertie," she replied with perilous candor, "I *like* spending money."

As I say, Mother was an early Keynesian.

Up until 1929, everything was coming up roses for the Forbeses, but by the end of the Depression we knew that the magazine was hanging on by its teeth, kept alive only by Dad's columning paycheck. We didn't suffer seriously, but were sharply aware of those tough times.

I saw my father cry only once. It was the morning that Duncan, then sixteen, was killed in an automobile accident. Bruce, having just turned seventeen and thus driver-licensable, had acquired a secondhand Model A Ford convertible that he had been ardently, arduously earning money to pay for by running a weekend car wash with some buddies at our garage at home. This tragic Sunday, he and Duncan were driving to Yama Farms, a lovely Adirondacks resort where our parents were staying for the weekend. As they rounded a curve on the Storm King Highway, the road was blocked by a flat-tired car, alongside which another car had pulled up to help. Bruce swerved, his car overturned and Duncan was killed instantly from a broken neck.

I went up to see my father, and he was sitting on the side of his bed, sobbing. I'd never seen him cry before. It really shook me. It wasn't that he was hard, because in his own way he was very gentle. He loved to do nice things, but I'd always thought of him as granite strong.

My father never lost his Scottish burr. It was only when we got a little older that we were even aware he had a burr, but he did, until the day he died.

He so loved to go back to his Scottish homeland that part of our growing up was to vacation in Aberdeenshire every other year. Often we'd sail on the Anchor Line from New York to its United Kingdom terminal up the Clyde in Glasgow. The highlight of those trips was the picnic

1987/1988: We revive B.C.'s New Deer Picnics fifty years after the last one he attended.

my father would give on the grounds of his old Whitehill, New Deer school, with all his surviving contemporaries and relatives from the area, along with their children and the rest of the kids currently enrolled. Shiny shillings and sixpences were the prizes for winners of sack races, three-legged races, dashes, tugs-of-war, et al. My brothers and I would all compete in the games and the races, but only Bruce ever bested the Aberdonian contemporaries. Bags of sticky bright candies containing pennies and halfpennies were dispensed to all the kids, while the elders devoured and sipped high tea. How my father loved these comings together of all those New Deerians so dear in his memory.

So we grew up accustomed to this Aberdeen stronghold of the Forbes clan. We virtually took Scotland for granted. It was no stranger to us, not a far or distant or different land. As we grew up, we felt—as well as were—kin to all things Scottish.

Then World War II broke out and there were no more ships plying the Atlantic to Great Britain or anywhere else. Dad resumed his visits

after the war as promptly as transatlantic shipping resumed, but by that time I had married and we siblings were all leading different lives. I didn't make it back to Scotland until just a few years ago, when I motorcycled around but did not try to look up any relatives. I just enjoyed reminiscing and touring the area, seeing a little bit of what I'd grown up with.

My father died in 1954, and two years ago I thought that in memory of him, and in honor of the approaching seventieth anniversary of the magazine, we should revive the New Deer picnics. All those years after the war he would go there alone, with none of his family to go with him while we were all knee-deep in our own lives, wives and children. Everybody—my two remaining brothers and my children—agreed that reviving the B. C. Forbes picnic was a fine idea, so in 1987 we hosted the first renewal of what we have resolved will be an annual affair.

My father was not buried in Scotland originally, because my mother had a plot for him in a cemetery in Englewood. He was a rock-hard Scottish Presbyterian, and she was a full-of-faith Catholic. Discussion of the relative merits of the two religions was totally forbidden. On the rare occasions discussion broke out, the comments tended to be furious because my fa-

ther felt the Pope was the devil and my mother thought she'd go to the devil because she'd married a Protestant heathen.

Though love had conquered all for twenty-eight years, by the time he died my father and mother had separated, but here he was in a Catholic cemetery, where Duncan was also buried. Despite their differences, having him in Englewood meant something to my mother while she was alive.

But now my brothers Wally and Gordon and I felt that Dad so loved going home that—if the remains mean anything to the gone—he would be happy to be back in Scotland on a permanent basis.

So last summer brother Wally and I, with two of his children, one of my sons and my daughter, and six of my seven granddaughters, brought B.C. back to St. Kane's Kirk in New Deer, to the churchyard he now shares with his blacksmith grandfather, James Moir.

MORE THAN I DREAMED • 45

The day before, we had concluded long negotiations to acquire the ruins of a venerable and famous Scottish castle called Pitsligo that had been built by Sir William Forbes in the early fifteenth century, together with three acres of land overlooking the North Sea and a small fishing village. The castle had played a glorious part in Scottish history, though Pitsligo hadn't belonged to a Forbes since the 1745 Rebellion. It had been a ruin for two hundred years, and ruins get ruined-er. We're not going to restore the castle. Instead we plan to stabilize what's left, leaving what tumbled where it rests, and green-grassing the rest of the grounds.

For us it's a real joy to think that Pitsligo, which my father grew up in terrific awe of, is now back in the Forbes clan, thanks to his bairns.

Last year's picnic, which followed Dad's reinterment, was better attended than ever. We visited yet again the house where he was born, which we're also negotiating to acquire. At the end of the day we flew the elephant hot-air balloon that we used in Thailand over the roofs of New Deer.

The services for my father were a mighty emotional event for our friends, but a happy day for Clan Forbes. It was the only joyful funeral I've ever been to—B.C., from the plains of Buchan to the towers of New York and finally home again.

Father used to say, "Son, what's the answer to ninety-nine questions out of a hundred? Money." He also said that business was originated to produce happiness and not to pile up millions, and I can honestly say I've taken him at his word.

He said that one should use money to be happy, but he couldn't quite do it himself, he couldn't quite shake that Scottish aspect of his heritage. He wasn't selfish, but neither was he comfortable about spending in a big way. Doubtless the undertakings described and colorfully depicted on the pages that follow have given him a turn or two.

For here's a tale of toy boats and real yachts; of soaring regular hot-air balloons and balloons of extraordinary shapes; of multiple motorcycles that have taken us throughout our land and many others; of fetes and collections; of home and other homes; of doings and things that I never dreamed of until shortly before they became real.

My inheritance of a sense of thrift is there, but not spectacularly so. While I fill a daily "round file," i.e. wastebasket, full of what was attached to them, paper clips themselves I save. I always turn out the lights behind me in empty rooms. With the edge of the toothbrush I get absolutely the last drop from any tube. But all together a lifetime of such savings probably hasn't financed much of what follows.

I am an ardent disciple of the school of thought that postulates you must spend money to make money. How you get it in the first place, so that you can make it multiply, is indeed a sort of chicken-and-egg situation.

For me, though, it wasn't so hard.

My father had started our business, and he wasn't mad at me when he died.

Tombstone of James Moir, B.C.'s grandfather; now both share the same ground at St. Kane's Kirk, New Deer, 1988.

New Deer, 1988: If the remains mean any-thing to the gone—B.C. would be glad to be back in Scotland on a permanent basis.

Forbes bairns, Pitsligo Castle, 1988.

Pitsligo Castle, returned to the Clan. Top Row (L–R): Elizabeth, Sabina, Moira, Alden, Cindy, MF, Wally, Alexandra, and Kip. Front Row (L–R): Charlotte, Sabina, Ken, Roberta, Catherine, and Moira.

The first Highlander. *Length: 72 feet. In service: 1955–1957.*

The second Highlander. *Length: 98 feet. In service: 1957–1967.*

The third Highlander. *Length: 117 feet. In service: 1967–January 1980.* RIGHT: *The third* Highlander's *flaming end, January 16, 1980.*

The fourth Highlander. *Length: 126 feet. In service: 1980–Fall 1985.*

The fifth Highlander. *Length: 151 feet. In service: October 23, 1985.*

CHAPTER

2

MESSING
ABOUT
IN BOATS

MANY OF US have a Rosebud lurking in our past—a toy train, a truck, a doll, or, like Citizen Kane, a sled. In the Forbes family, toy boats were more prized than electric trains or other playthings. We were forever sailing them in local brooks and streams, and in summers on lakes and oceans. Not a one survived to be part of our collection, but the memory of them and the joy of them account for its formation.

me from the very beginning. I can remember the first time I sailed on an ocean monarch at the age of seven. It was the *Aquitania*, one of the great old four-stack Cunarders. Almost every other summer until World War II, our family used to sail to Great Britain, oft times directly to Glasgow, on the Anchor Line, other times to Southhampton, via Cunard or White Star. From Scotland we would go to Europe, and we'd sail home from Le Havre or Marseilles.

On one crossing I took a toy boat and, with my brother's aid, lowered it—secured by a strong twine—the long way from rail to sea. We intended that this toy liner too should make the

Wind-up toy ocean liner by Fleischmann (Germany), 1955.

I cannot pinpoint exactly when this fascination with boats began, but I do remember from early on being totally engrossed in the bathtub with what used to be called in those days "talcum tugs." I used to go to the medicine cabinet and take the lids off all the containers that were big enough to float. Then, making waves, I'd imagine storms at sea and log which of my makeshift armada stayed afloat the longest.

So boats and water had a strong appeal for

Atlantic crossing. It survived departure from the dock, but within a few minutes of our being under way the bashing soon saw it under way to Davey Jones's locker. I lost it, but in spirit it may have led to the start of my toy boat collection.

I didn't collect toy boats when I was a kid, I *played* with them. I *loved* toy boats. And it's clear to me that more than anything else it is nostalgia that sparked both the toy boat and the

PREVIOUS PAGE: *Three stalwarts in the other Forbes armada.*

"The Malcolm S. Forbes Family" by John Koch, 1956. L–R: Bob, Bertie, Moira, Steve, Kip, Tim and MF.

toy soldier collections—the warm, embracing memories of the endless fun we had with them.

One of those transatlantic crossings I mentioned comes to mind with special clarity. Nine-year-old brother Duncan and I were the bane of the ship's elevator operators. We used to push the buzzer for them on A deck, then run down to E deck and ring again, then race back up to A. The elevator operators soon got to know us, and within the first two days, as you may imagine, we became extremely unpopular with these fellows.

I remember one night when we were going down to dinner in the elevator—in those days everybody dressed for dinner, and my father was decked out in his black tie and my mother looked ravishing—and the operator said, "Mr. Forbes, these boys are driving me crazy." Mother was mortified.

That absolutely put an end to our little game. Dad told us at the dinner table that if he heard one more such complaint we were in deep trouble. And when my father used to say "deep trouble," there were definite visions of spankings.

We seemed to have had a hard time though

staying good on the high seas. On the return trip, we sailed from France on the Dollar liner *President Hayes*, one of what was probably the biggest passenger fleet in the United States in those days, headed by Stanley R. Dollar. For some reason, my brother and I thought it would be exciting to create the impression that the ship had sunk. We found items with the ship's name on them—life preservers, pillows, anything that would float—and in the dark of night tossed the whole lot overboard. We figured a passing ship would recover them and think the *Hayes* had gone to the bottom.

But it was our bottoms which suffered. When the stewards were taking inventory at the end of the trip, they found that all these things were missing and came, again, to discuss our seagoing deportment with my parents. In addition to the spankings we got, modest allowances were encumbered for a long time—until accounts were settled to the Dollar Line's satisfaction.

Early on I started asking for toy boats for Christmas, birthdays or Easter. Actually, I was torn between a toy soldier set and a toy boat. Toy boats were quite expensive, everything being relative, but with the smaller ones of six, eight, ten, or twelve inches I could play for hours on the rug, dreaming I was sailing the oceans of the world.

About half a mile from our house, which was on the outskirts of Englewood, there were fields, and across a dirt road lay woods that extended all the way up to the Englewood Cliffs. At its base ran a busy brook. There we'd launch our little tin ocean liners and let the current take them along while we followed. When they'd encounter branches or obstacles, or the current was too strong, one of the boats might capsize and sink, and then we would have to decide whether we were going to make a major disaster of it and mourn the drowned, or retrieve it, shake it out and continue as if nothing had happened.

The longest voyage the boats could make without portage was to the Devil's Hole, our local swimming hole. For our tiny navy, that was the end of the line.

When I went away to camp—I think I was about nine years old—I would float tin cans and build a little fire of pinecones on board, imagining these were ocean liners steaming along.

In later summers, vacationing with the family at Belgrade Lakes in Maine, my brothers and I would each save our money to rent rowboats. When we were a bit older and a little more solvent, we added outboard motors to them. We would spend day after day just exploring every perimeter of the lakes.

Steve's twins, Sabina and Roberta, performing a routine seaworthiness drill.

Three Bing Leviathans *(Germany); 1916–1920.*

Falk Oceanliners: MF found the one in the right front in F.A.O. Schwarz's antique toy department and started the collection.

Small ocean liner by Bing (Germany), 1920.

More than bubbles in a granddaughter's tub.

So our wondrous toy boat collection springs from the memory of childhood fantasies related to almost anything that floated. Happily, but perhaps not surprisingly, my own children grew up loving to play with boats. The collection didn't get started with that end in mind, however. It began when I spotted an antique toy boat at F.A.O. Schwarz—a fabulous boat of a size I never as a boy had the means to possess, perhaps twenty-four or thirty inches long, really magnificent—and I bought it for quite a large amount of money. Soon after, at an auction where I was bidding on toy soldiers, a few tin toy boats showed up, and I couldn't resist buying them.

Within a year of this fresh awareness, and the fun of finally being able to have more toy boats than I'd ever dreamed of, we ran out of shelf space in the kids' playroom. I continued to add more and often joined the children playing with them in pool and pond at home—until the realization grew that the steadily climbing prices I was paying were removing these from the toys-to-be-played-with category. They were harder to find, too. It seemed all of a sudden that we had become toy boat collectors.

What had started as toys to play with in bathtubs, brooks and lakes had turned into something else entirely. Today the Forbes armada, anchored at Fifth Avenue and Twelfth Street in New York, embraces some five hundred vessels, most of them in their original, unrestored condition, made of tin and cast iron and powered by clockwork, steam, batteries and a lot of nostalgia.

The best of them come from toy boats' golden

Warship by Bing, L'Antonio, 1910.

Schiffe

in modernster Ausführung, **mit solidem Uhrwerk.** Hochfein lackiert, reichste Ausstattung.

10.31/6

10.31 6 Ozeandampfer, 42 cm lang, mit 2 Rettungsbooten . . . . per Stück Mk.

10.38/2

10.38.1 Ozeandampfer, 42 cm lang, mit 4 Rettungsbooten . . . . per Stück Mk.
2   do.   50 „   „   6   „   . . . . „   „   „

— 51 —

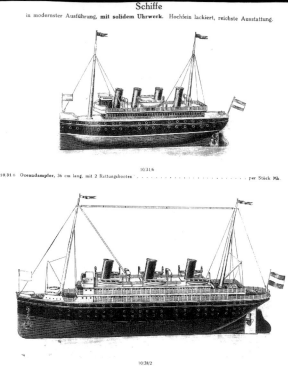

Page from Bing catalog, 1912.

age—from around 1870 to 1955. This was the period during which the most beautiful and magical of these very special tin playthings were manufactured by firms with names like Marklin, Bing, Carette, Arnold, Falk and Fleischmann, the great toymakers of Nuremberg; Maltête & Parent, Radiguet and JEP of France; and Ives, Orkin, Brown and James Fallows & Co. in this country.

Though not strictly a toy, this Silver Presentation Paddle Steamer *is special. Made by Fabergé for the Volga Shipbuilders who presented it to Czar Nicholas' only son, Alexis, in 1913, the boat contains a music box.*

In both of these Fabergé frames the Czarevitch sports a hatband with the name of the Imperial yacht, Standard.

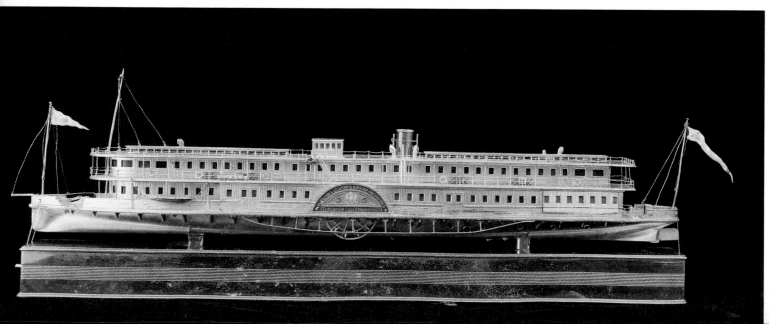

This Belle Epoque French craft from Radiguet runs on steam and has small shootable brass cannons.

A top U.S. toy maker in the twenties, Ives, produced this charming Sally.

Bowsprit by Maltête & Parent (France), 1900.

Lost in the world of Marklin's Mauretania.

Bing's biggest bathtub beauty: the forty inch Leviathan.

They range from an eight-and-a-half-inch key-wound metal speedboat that was sold for seventy-nine cents in 1912 by Sears, Roebuck, to $28,600 paid at auction for a wind-up *Lusitania*, made by the German firm Marklin, around 1908; and the flagship of the fleet, the Silver Presentation Paddle Steamer, made in 1913 by Fabergé as a present to Czarevitch Alexis, the only son of Czar Nicholas II. Now worth far more than the $31,000 we paid 13 years ago, it has a hidden music box that plays "Sailing Down the Volga" and "God Save the Czar."

Why are old toy boats so relatively rare these days? Because they survived less than other toys for the very same reasons that real boats survive less long than most other manufactured things. Toy boats differ from models in that they were not individually crafted but manufactured for a large market. Toy boats were meant to be played with. They sailed into the waves, rusted in their boxes, sank or blew up. And as with the real ones, the more toy boats did their thing, the less likely they were to survive.

Sadly, no child plays with these toys any-more. They are too fragile and too expensive, so most of them are locked up in collections like ours. Still, it would be a melancholy affair to look at toy boats by yourself, and sharing the fun of the boats with a new generation of bathtub admirals is perhaps almost as pleasurable as remembering, for me, how it all began.

MF at the helm of Wings, *early 1950s.*

Wings *at dockside, Labrador.*

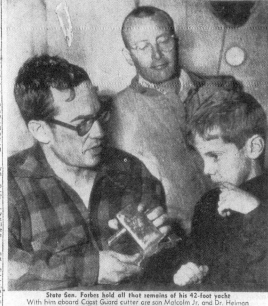
Wings *clipped in hurricane; September 6, 1953.*

I think I have always thought of our sequence of Forbes *Highlanders* as true descendants of our enthusiasm for toy boats.

Before we had these company-owned larger yachts, I had a couple of personal ones. When our children were little I bought a secondhand thirty-foot Owens cruiser, which we kept near the head of the Raritan River, right opposite Rutgers University. It was the nearest yacht basin to our Far Hills, New Jersey, home.

I had never skippered a boat before I bought that one. You don't need a license to captain a boat, you know—all you need is a boat. I didn't know how to read buoys or charts, and I remember learning my basic seamanship while going down the Raritan. It was quite a long ride

down the Raritan that first time, with my wife and three children, reading up on buoys and the difference between red and black ones; learning to decipher charts and keep from going aground.

Boat lovers suffer a disease: biggerboatitis. It is seldom terminal, but it's a long time before size seizure ceases. So by and by I bought a forty-two foot Chris-Craft, also secondhand, that I literally lost at sea and then eventually recovered again, all on a fabulous trip that began as a weekend journey up the Hudson River.

I had my oldest son, Steve, with me. He was then six going on seven, and together we sailed up the Hudson, through the Albany locks, and through the waterway to Lake Champlain. I'd never been in locks before, and I wasn't very good at it. But that's a whole tale in itself. As things turned out, instead of coming back when the weekend was over, we left the boat at the farthest point we'd reached and flew back. From then on I spent the summer rigging up three-day weekends and flying back up with friends.

I'd been told that one thing you couldn't do in a boat like mine was go down the St. Lawrence and sail on to Labrador. So, of course, I immediately wanted to go to Labrador. I'd read about Labrador and it sounded intriguing. I was fascinated by the idea. "Gee, just imagine, in my little boat we could go all the way to Labrador."

And so we did.

I'd been warned that the only gas available from the little villages along the way was fisherman-type diesel, too thick for the engines we had on the Chris-Craft. But when you're igno-

Wings *in the Albany locks.*

rant of reality you often ignore it, and we all got to Labrador using fisherman gas. But then in Sydney, Nova Scotia, on the way back, we had to have the engines rebuilt, and thereby lies another tale of how we lost the boat in a hurricane. We got it back later, but I sold her at the end of the season.

Then came the idea of using a boat for company entertaining. As mentioned earlier, I had taken over as editor-in-chief after my father died, and my older brother Bruce was handling the business end as president.

I had been reading all the yachting magazines and had seen advertised a converted Canadian Navy vessel, a wooden-hulled seventy-two-footer that had been converted into a pleasure boat. I think the price may have been around $40,000. Anyway, I couldn't afford it on my salary. It needed a captain and probably one other crewman as well.

I went to brother Bruce and said, "You know, if we buy this as a company, we can use it to entertain people and have the fun of owning it." He took a little persuading, because he was subject to getting seasick. He wasn't as fond of the sea as I was. But he was a great friend of Red Blaik, the fabled football coach at West Point, and he realized that with it he could take potential advertisers up the Hudson to Army football games. From that angle, he saw the usefulness of it. I saw even more use in terms of going down the Inland Waterway in the wintertime to Florida, and even getting over to the Bahamas, and together we wound up deciding to buy our first company yacht.

We called her the *Highlander*, and she turned out to be a great success. But it took a lot of maintenance, and there were limitations as to how many people we could carry—only six or eight even for a day trip, which most of our entertaining consisted of. So we began looking in the magazines for yet another, and bigger, yacht.

We found one that sounded perfect. The boat was in Athens and I flew over to negotiate. She was a ninety-eight-foot Feadship, with two masts and sails. Essentially it was a motor yacht, with an alleged sailing capability. The

The Highlander *that started it all; 1955–1957.*

The launching of the second Highlander *at the De Vries Shipyard at Aalsmeer, Holland; November 16, 1957.*

owner was a Greek shipowner, but on a considerably smaller scale than Niarchos or Onassis. He and his wife had decided they were going to build a new and bigger yacht, so they were offering this one for sale.

I made a deal with him and cabled home to report success. But by the time I returned, the day after, there was a message that said his wife had decided that he might not live long enough to build a new one, so they were going to keep the old yacht, even though he'd signed a contract with me.

Keenly disappointed, I found out who their architect was and tracked him down at the De Vries Shipyard in Aalsmeer, just outside Amsterdam. He turned out to be Mr. Fritz de Voogt, chief architect for the Dutch Navy. He agreed to draw up new plans for a yacht similar to the one we didn't get, but without the masts that would have made it impossible for us to pass under the various Harlem bridges during our sails around Manhattan.

Thus the second *Highlander* came to be, on November 16, 1957. She served us well for about ten years. Because she proved to be so popularly successful for beguiling big-business guests, we decided to build a larger new one. At 117 feet, the third *Highlander* lasted us for thirteen years, until she burned at the dock of the Jockey Club in North Miami.

As I wrote in an editorial obit in *Forbes*, it was clear that boats had become a very vital part of our doing business at the magazine. So after the fire I called the same shipyard, expecting it would be two years or more before we'd be back on the seas. We were elated to learn that they had available a just-completed yacht they had built for a Connecticut gentleman that was 9 feet larger than the just burned *Highlander*.

The owner had a problem because, after she was built, President Jimmy Carter had signed a new tax bill that would end expense-account lunches and also scuttle the corporate use of yachts for tax-deductible business entertaining.

We flew down to St. Thomas, where she was on charter, to check her out. She was just right for us, so we bought the fourth *Highlander*.

The second Highlander; *a fair wind and a following sea.*

The launching of the third Highlander; *new boat, same shipyard; March 1967.*

My editorial in Forbes, *February 18, 1980.*

A DEATH IN THE FAMILY

TWENTY-FOUR YEARS AGO we commissioned the building of the third Forbes *Highlander*, and two years later this lovely ship began its lifetime of service to this company. Between 1967 and the *Highlander*'s flaming end on January 16, 1980, resulting from an accidental galley fire, countable thousands of America's corporate Consequentials—and often their ladies—came to know and love her, as did Kings and Prime Ministers and Presidents, foreign and domestic.

Perhaps it's not an exaggeration to say that from *Highlander* conversations were generated more articles than from any other ship since Noah's ark and Christopher Columbus' wee fleet. Uncountable *Forbes* stories of business, businesses and the men who run them were born aboard her. In several instances, major American corporate mergers resulted from friendships formed on the *Highlander*. As Marsh & McLennan Chairman Patton Kline wrote, "The *Highlander* meant more to American business than any other vessel in the world."

This *Highlander* will remain a cherished memory to all the thousands who sailed on her.

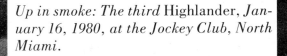

COVER: Motor Boating & Sailing *Magazine; November 1979.*

Up in smoke: The third Highlander, *January 16, 1980, at the Jockey Club, North Miami.*

Even though entertaining on boats would no longer be allowed as deductible expenses, the *Highlanders* had become too valuable to sacrifice, even though it meant operating them with after tax dollars.

Wonderful as our "off-the-shelf" *Highlander* was, we kept in mind the idea of building another, designed to our own specifications. What we needed was a boat where large numbers of people could enjoy, relax and not be crowded elbow to elbow.

I had heard about the work of Jon Bannenberg, Britain's top yacht designer, and I visited him in London to discuss ideas for the new yacht. What he came up with was totally fabulous. I was excited by the conception and bowled over with the reality. It exceeded our fondest hopes. The Bannenberg *Highlander* sets the design and interior direction where all yachts of major size will be in future years.

The interior he came up with is dramatic—not plushly opulent—with spaces not chopped off from each other. It's amazing how she soaks up people, yet is thoroughly cozy if only a few people are on board.

Though I've joked that the fourth *Highlander* was sold "because the ashtrays were full," the truth is that she was no longer adequate for the numbers we were entertaining. Though we have all the high-tech amenities—two big 900 HP diesels, two 140-kilowatt generators with a standby, two radars, satellite navigation, two gyro systems, a weather fax machine, a helicopter and two super speedboats (a Cigarette and a Donzi)—basically all the *Highlanders* have been party platforms that give us a chance to wine, dine and get a handle on the VIPs we write about for the magazine. And as Forbes Inc. keeps getting bigger, the parties keep getting bigger and the boats have kept getting bigger.

The *Highlanders* have been the hardest-working yachts in America. Since our business is to know the nation's movers and shakers—so that we can evaluate if they should be shaken, moved or removed—the yacht offers a great ex-

The fourth Highlander.

cuse to entrap high-level executives for a few hours. At *Forbes* we put more stock in evaluating a chief executive than we do in reporting quarterly earnings. With the *Highlanders*, we get a chance to size up the people the magazine covers editorially, and as a publisher, we get a chance on other occasions to sell our guests on the virtues of advertising in *Forbes*.

The increasingly influential young advertising agency planners who decide what publica-

The fifth Highlander, *shortly after its arrival in New York City; April 8, 1986. At the time, we were said to be ordering a new* Highlander *because the ashtrays on the old one were full. The truth is, the fourth was no longer adequate for the numbers we were entertaining; and besides, it was time for a helicopter aboard.*

tions are used also like going to sea. Recent research by ad agency Lord, Geller, Federico, Einstein, reports *The New York Times,* found that ". . . media planners were influenced first by circulation data available through computer information banks and then by events sponsored by publishers and broadcasters. The Lord, Geller survey also turned up the fact that the perquisite young planners found most memorable was a ride on Malcolm Forbes' yacht."

Ninety-nine percent of the *Highlander*'s use is for business. It's an enjoyable way to work— and effective *because* it's enjoyable. We keep a pretty busy schedule: at least three events for fifty to a hundred or so people a week from May to October; lunch and dinner cruises around New York Harbor; excursions up the Hudson to Army football games in the fall, and then, in the winter, we ferry visiting executives around Florida ports near the major golf courses.

Often we're asked by State Department friends to host—and sometimes we invite on our own—prime ministers, heads of state, kings, queens and princes, people who are consequential on the international scene. We also entertain political figures, not on a partisan basis, but influential people in the government —usually on the national level but often on state and city levels too. We also invite corporate heads—say, the head of a major chain store or of a company like Procter & Gamble— who don't represent potential business for *Forbes* but are deemed important to us as news sources.

On a yacht like the *Highlander* you can establish the kind of rapport you don't achieve talking across a desk. It's a whole other atmosphere, and when you get a good group together there's bound to be not sparks flying, but lively conversation. There have been times when corporate takeover rivals have slugged things out verbally between courses at dinner. I don't plan things that way, naturally, but sometimes it happens because of long-standing invitations.

Sometimes I get into hot water myself. I remember well a leisurely cruise up the Hudson with King Hussein of Jordan en route to a dinner at then Governor Nelson Rockefeller's Tarrytown estate. I was asking about the tension Jordan was involved in, and some questions went to the core.

The grand salon with Bannenberg's signature leather ceiling.

The afterdeck sports shipmodel dioramas.

A cutaway view of the present Highlander.

A champagne welcome for our new Highlander, *October 23, 1985.*

Always aboard: two Harleys for the high seas.

As the discussion wore on, the King began addressing me with ever-increasing use of "sir." I thought he was extraordinarily polite—until I got the inside dope from Henry Kissinger: the more times King Hussein said "sir," the more annoyed he was.

No one would ever say that the *Highlander* comes under the category of necessary transportation. When people admire the *Highlander*, I have to agree with Huckleberry Finn that "there warn't no home like a raft. Other places do seem so cramped up and smothery, but a raft don't. You feel mighty free and easy and comfortable on a raft."

As a good Scotsman, I can appreciate that none of us is above a free drink and a good meal —araft or ashore.

MF on his bowsprit reading perch.

Laucala: *Below deck.*

A while after we acquired our coconut Bali-h'ai, *Laucala*, in Fiji (see page 198), I set out to find the perfect-for-our-purposes motor sailor that could be used to bring guests and a reasonable amount of cargo to and from Fiji's International Airport at Nadi or its capital of Suva, and Laucala. Finding the fit I had in mind took a lot of looking over many months, but we found it on the French Riviera.

Promptly christened the LAUCALA, this German-built 76-foot, five-cabined yawl sailed to Tangier, where our design genius, Robert Gerofi, Director of Forbes Palais Mendoub, saw to the interior refitting while the HIGHLANDER's captain, Alexander Pfotenhauer, made the vessel ready for its Atlantic crossing. With Capt. Alex, son Robert, and five others, the crew and I made a twenty-day crossing via the Azores to English Harbor. By the tenth day, I sorely missed the news and was frustrated by the frequent inability to communicate with New York. But there was compensation in lying on the sail-shrouded bowsprit and reading, with only the slapping of the waves and occasional performances by dolphins, to interrupt (or rather contribute to) this out-of-this-world reverie.

After extensive preparations, the LAUCALA headed for its 8,000-mile journey to Laucala, though I only got to accompany it on the leg from the Atlantic side of the Panama Canal to the Galapagos Islands off the coast of Ecuador. But the LAUCALA's uses didn't develop as anticipated and mostly sitting for nearly two years in this paradise's harbor wasn't totally conducive to either the crew or the ship's elan.

Aside from the monotonously uneventful Atlantic crossing, I'd never done much actual "sailing." But in the back of my mind, I'd harbored the possibility of going around the world on her, and since we decided to bring the LAUCALA home, I thought it would be a start to take the first leg from Fiji to Auckland, New Zealand, where I'd planned to motor from the top end of kiwi-land to Dunedin at the lower end.

So, with all the aplomb of the unsalted, I mustered a crew and pushed off—into prevailing winds that blew in the opposite direction. After eight punishing days of endless tacking and beating—and I do mean beating—by head winds, we finally inched our way into the nearest New Zealand harbor, where I abandoned ship.

Literally.

Long since over the side had gone my around-the-world-by-sail fantasies. I had the LAUCALA shipped to Miami from Auckland, and sold it to the first serious bidder.

RIGHT: *The* Laucala *under sail, over the bounty.*

At the suggestion of the State Department, Bertie and I were delighted on the evening of September 30, 1976, to entertain President and Mrs. William R. Tolbert, Jr., of Liberia for a dinner and harbor cruise aboard the *Highlander*. Along with some cabinet members and other factotums of his government, the long-time Liberian President was on an official state visit.

In a unique expression of appreciation, the next morning at their suite in the Waldorf Towers the President installed and berobed me as "Paramount Chief of the Nimba tribe." His wife garbed mine with proper regalia and accoutrements befitting a paramount chief's mate.

A few weeks later I had a letter from "my" Nimba tribe chief-on-the-scene saying that our village was some 11 miles from the nearest proper road and would I be kind enough to provide a connecting road.

Forty-two months later several of our Liberian *Highlander* guests, including Tolbert and Cecil Dennis, were literally shot at the stake in a bloody revolution by Liberian soldiers who'd resented being ruled by former American slaves since the nation's founding. They and their descendants had been the reigning elite until present ruler, Samuel K. Doe, Commander in Chief, as a sergeant overthrew and killed them.

President Nicolae Ceauşescu of Romania with MF and Kip Forbes on board the Highlander. *October 18, 1970.*

H.R.H. The Duke of Gloucester with Kip. October 11, 1974.

MF and Bertie entertaining Prime Minister and Mrs. Hedi Nouira of Tunisia in the main salon. May 5, 1975.

MF with President Dr. Urho Kekkonen of Finland. July 31, 1976.

Steve Forbes with Ratu Sir Kamisese Mara, Prime Minister of Fiji and Adi Lady Lala Mara. October 10, 1976.

The Prime Minister of Fiji at the helm.

MF with the Prime Minister of Turkey and Mrs. Bülent Ecevit. He was jailed by his successor. June 3, 1978.

MF and Steve with H.M. King Hussein of Jordan. April 28, 1977.

MF with the Prime Minister of Japan and Mrs. Zenko Suzuki, Ambassador Mike Mansfield and Arnold Palmer. May 5, 1981.

Bertie entertaining H.R.H. The Prince of Wales, First Lady Nancy Reagan and Mayor Ed Koch. June 17, 1981.

Portrait of Queen Elizabeth II and Prince Philip to MF, 1976.

Brittania—*taken from the* High-lander *enroute to Newport, Rhode Island. July 10, 1976.*

H.I.H. Crown Prince Naruhito of Japan. October 19, 1985.

MF and Kip with His Excellency Dato' Seri Dr. Mahathir Bin Mohamad, Prime Minister of Malaysia. September 27, 1986.

MF greets Mme. Danielle Mitterand at the Highlander, during the Statue of Liberty's centennial re-unveiling. July 4, 1986.

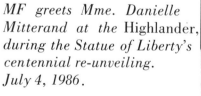

His Excellency General Prem Tinsulanonda, Prime Minister of Thailand with MF. October 7, 1987.

MF, honored at dinner by Secretary of State Schultz, greets incoming Secretary of State James Baker and wife Susan. November 2, 1988.

Then Vice President George Bush inspects the Highlander **with Bob, Steve and MF, Washington, D.C. April 30, 1987.**

The Great Amazonian Expedition

Some people say they wonder why I do the things I do—the hot-air ballooning across America, the motorcycling through Europe and Asia with the "Capitalist Tools" with specially shaped hot-air balloons. In truth, the world is not so much my oyster as my Everest. It is, simply, *there* in all its global diversity.

But going up the Amazon, even in a 151-foot motor yacht, was a daunting proposition. For me, the Amazon has always had a mystique about it—a sublimely forbidding quality. And I am not alone. I had followed closely the adventures of Daniel K. Ludwig, a two-billion-dollar forest-to-paper development effort, including towing a paper mill and power plant upriver by sea from Japan. And Henry Ford had tried a rubber plantation there in the '20s—a total wipe-out.

But I was also intrigued by Jacques Cousteau's trek through the Amazon in 1983, and it may have been his adventure that finally inspired us to take *The Highlander* up the Amazon waterway in 1987. Times change, of course, but even with encroaching development by the Brazilian government, the Amazon basin is still a stern frontier.

As for our Amazon expedition, Christopher Buckley's delightful chronicle in Condé Nast's *Traveler* says it best.

RIGHT: *From the helicopter, the 151 foot* Highlander *gives scale to the vastness of the mighty Amazon.*

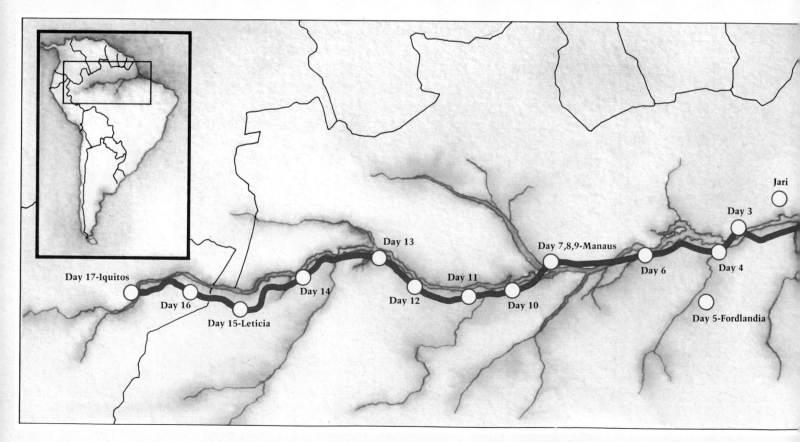

Jari

Day 3

Day 13

Day 7,8,9-Manaus

Day 4

Day 17-Iquitos

Day 16

Day 14

Day 11

Day 6

Day 12

Day 10

Day 15-Leticia

Day 5-Fordlandia

Belem

Day 2

Day 1

On the tarmac at Manaus.

Fellow travelers: the Highlander *and the* Virginian.

Returning from shore leave.

EXCERPTS FROM JOURNAL
CHRISTOPHER BUCKLEY

DAY ONE

On way from Newark (freezing) to Manaus (steambath) aboard Forbes's Boeing 727, *The Capitalist Tool*, I read aloud to company from Alex Shoumatoff's remarkable book *The Rivers Amazon*. Contains graphic medical descriptions of various ways Amazon can ruin your entire day—including nose dropping off, blindness from insects crapping in eyeball—and memorable section on toothpick-size catfish with fondness for "mammalian orifices," which must be surgically removed.

"Unh," says someone.

Am about to move on to snakes and furry arachnids, but am told to shut up.

We land. *The Highlander* and *The Virginian* are waiting at the dock in Manaus, guarded by men with shotguns. Glenn Ellison, *The Highlander*'s second steward, pipes us aboard with bagpipes.

Forbes—hereinafter, Malcolm—gives us the Cook's tour: The topmost deck is a solarium, as if a *bateau-mouche* had been grafted on top. There are four guest suites in addition to Malcolm's master suite, with its whirlpool and steambath and Spanish-galleon rear picture window. I draw Burgundy. Others are Blue, White, and Gray. The king of Bulgaria says, "It's clever. This way no one is offended by being given 'Cabin Number Four.' "

After dinner our omnicompetent guide, Silvio Barros, gives us a brief sketch of what's ahead. Tomorrow we'll see the famous Manaus opera house, built by the rubber barons at the turn of the century, when Manaus was booming. Contrary to popular legend, Enrico Caruso did not sing there. Silvio apologizes that no operas are being currently put on.

It's the perfect opera house," observes Kip. "You can see it but you can't hear it."

DAY TWO

We bus around Manaus. The public market, built by Eiffel, reeks of putrescent catfish. Vultures swarm over shantytowns. At the opera house we learn that after a military coup in the seventies, the military government decreed that the beautiful rose-colored building be painted —gray, to conform with all official buildings. The kings of Greece and Bulgaria, having extensive experience of the military mind, shake their heads.

A buffet is spread at the Hotel Tropical. We're given drinks made of *cachaça*—napalm-strength sugarcane rum—and passion fruit. Eyeballs poached, we eat grilled local fish, *tucunaré*. For dessert, a manioc pudding with cloves. "Let's hope the prussic acid has been leached out," says the king of Bulgaria, diving in.

Glenn Ellison and "The Meeting of the Waters."

We cross the Rio Negro, a major Amazonian tributary, and hike a short distance into the jungle to Salvador Lake.

Lucky Roosevelt to Malcolm: "You know, Archie's grandfather died of his trip to Brazil. He caught a fever and he was never right after that."

The appearance of a three-foot-long crocodilian inhibits immediate gleeful scampering into the lake, though everyone's faint with heat and soaked through with sweat. Lucky, Esteban, and Kip gamely jump in.

Archie: "They say alligators only take small pieces out of you."

Guide: "Yes, but sometimes the wrong pieces."

Later, during cocktails on *The Highlander*, Pat Kluge appears, stunning in crinkly white cotton shirt, with boa constrictor, Gus, coiled around her arms. Gus belongs to our *sous-chef*, David, and eats day-old chicks and mice. Mice hard to come by in Manaus. Rats plentiful, but generally too large for Gus to swallow.

Dinner of cold pear soup, tiny lamb chops, rosettes of baked mashed potato. Dessert is piped in by the steward to the tune of "The

Roughing it. Center foreground (L–R): MF, King Simeon of Bulgaria; (from left): King Constantine of Greece, John Kluge, Patricia Kluge, Esteban Ganoza, Christopher Buckley, Queen Anne-Marie of Greece, Lord and Lady Romsey, Queen Margarita of Bulgaria, Archibald Roosevelt, former U.S. Chief of Protocol Selwa Roosevelt, Kip Forbes.

Fellow travelers.

Green Hills of Tyrol": three sherbets garnished with mint leaves and candied violets, all inside brass incense pots from Thailand.

Kip explains his father was served petits fours inside these at a hotel in Thailand, with dry ice smoke pluming out the holes. He expresses disappointment because the Manaus dry ice factory was closed until tomorrow afternoon. "We'll just have to make do." Guests feel insulted and complain bitterly. After dinner, Cuban cigars courtesy of Hassan, king of Morocco, via diplomatic pouch, hence not illegal, Malcolm emphasizes.

The *Virginians* are piped ashore to "Auld Lang Syne." The passengers and crew of the Greek cruiser docked across from us are leaning over the rails to get a glimpse of the Greek king and queen. As Constantine returns their waves, the ship issues three deafening blasts from its stack—"Go with God" in marine signal language. The crowd roars, the scene suddenly charged and cinematic.

The big ship pulls out, eventually becoming a blazing wedding cake of strung lights in the distance. We watch it recede in the darkness.

"It's interesting," says Simeon. "Tino (the king) went aboard before dinner to have an ouzo with the crew. But the captain never showed up. So he thinks he must have views."

MF and young Amazonian confer on Brazil's foreign debt.

DAY THREE

Up early for canoe trip into jungle. Malcolm advises us to oil up against mosquito bites—the local variety is chloroquine-resistant—with something made by Avon (Ding-Dong) called Skin-So-Soft. It's a body lotion made for soft-skinned ladies, but apparently the malarial anopheles mosquitoes detest it.

"Who told you about this?" I ask, skeptical but nonetheless smearing myself all over.

"Nancy Pierpont."

"Who?"

Kip interjects, as Kip often does: "You know Nancy. She has a *great* sense of humor."

Above us we see a half-dozen monkeys of the "smelly'" macaque variety, but our nostrils are filled with the sweetness of *damas de noche* blossoms.

Back to the ship for Malcolm's press conference. He enters with Gus wrapped around his arm and assures twenty reporters that Brazil's $100 billion foreign debt will just have to be "restructured." (He does not add "because your government is inept." We are guests here.) The press greatly relieved. Front-page headline next day: "Forbes: No Crisis in Brazil."

DAY FOUR

We (finally) shove off. Ten miles downriver we pass from the cola-red of the Rio Negro into the café-au-lait of the Solimões, the river that will

River town.

Stilted living: The luxuriant river valley is difficult to farm during the rainy season.

Rush hour in Manaus.

carry us the 1,200 miles to Iquitos, with some help from the twin GM 900-horsepower diesel engines. The meeting of the two waters is dramatic. They don't mix for a long stretch, owing to differing density, speed, and coloration.

Glenn the bagpiper appears in full regalia at the bow to pipe us through to the tune, naturally, of "The Meeting of the Waters."

"Know why the waters don't mix?" asks Dr. Nunez. He is a young and friendly Brazilian specialist in tropical diseases who Malcolm thought it prudent to have along.

"Speed, density—"

"Racism," he smiles.

After lunch Kip and I inflate the wading pool we bought in the market at Manaus and splash about. The only thing the designer left out was a pool. We are three degrees under the equator, and the sun blazes hot—about 105 degrees at midday. After no more than fifteen minutes, skin turns pink. After thirty minutes, precancerous.

Later that afternoon, sitting in the fantail salon with the wonderful dioramas of whaling scenes and shipbuilding, I hear a bang-bang-BANG underneath. Should I tell the captain? Minutes later the crew are pulling up the floorboards and frowning. Half an hour later they're donning wet suits. Dr. Nunez, who has a bit of the perverse about him, watches them while calling out the names of various things they are apt to run into down there.

"Pirarucu!" he trills. These get up to ten feet, 250 pounds.

"*Piraiba*!" Six feet, 300 pounds.

"Piranha!" Small, but massively inconvenient.

We tender over for dinner with the *Virginians*, Lucky not altogether happy about bats diving in and out of flashlight beams. Kip clutches a catalog on the Forbes collection of Victoriana. "I thought King Constantine might be interested, since he's Victoria's great great-grandson." Simeon is related as well. My eyes fasten on a photograph of a huge pair of bloomers. Item number 44: "Personally Hers." I suppress the vulgar temptation to ask Kip what a pair of imperial bloomers goes for.

Lady Lucky Roosevelt braves the crocodiles, while the men brave the inflatable pool.

John Kluge shows us around. *The Virginian* used to be *The Highlander IV*, so Kip is familiar. John, like Malcolm, collects. An entire wall of beautiful and rare seashells. Also, various early U.S. Navy dirks and cutlasses; an arrow from the *Mary Rose*, Henry VIII's flagship; a letter from Nelson; a hammock hook from the U.S.S. *Constitution*. His other interests, past and present: *Cats* (22 percent); Ice Capades; Harlem Globetrotters; a collection of seventy-two carriages; serious quantities of art, including a personally financed ten-year project of "narrative art" entitled "Seven Lagoons"; Democratic party politics. John is the only Democrat I know worth $4 billion. Come to think of it, he is the only *person* I know worth $4 billion.

Kip talks about Trinchera Ranch, his father's place in Colorado. Originally 170,000 acres. "It was nice, because everything you could see from the house was ours. Then Pa bought an additional eighty-seven thousand acres and it was even nicer, because everything you saw from the plane was ours." I like Kip.

It dawns on me uneasily that I am the only one calling the king of Bulgaria Simeon.

DAY FIVE

Malcolm helicopters in from meeting with President Sarney.

"How was he?"

"In better shape than he should be." I take this as a reference to Brazil's foreign debt, now over $100 billion.

He showers and changes into a pair of extremely loud WASP-psychedelic-pink slacks with smiling lions heads and plays bridge with the Roosevelts and Kip.

I read Jacques Cousteau's enthralling book on his Amazon expedition. The river we are on has ten tributaries longer than the Mississippi, produces twelve times its outflow, and could fill Lake Ontario in three hours. *"Draw my lake, would you, Jeeves." "Very good, sir."*

The current here is swift, five knots, bringing huge trees that crash against hull at night, starting you awake. At first I wondered why the ship swerved so sharply at night; now I know why. The current also carries floating islands of *canarana* grass, which King Constantine and Lord Romsey shoot at with deer rifles.

Silvio arrives as we dive into butterscotch sundaes and says *The Virginian* has radioed. Some of them are planning to spend the night in the jungle.

"Why?" asks Malcolm. A *wise* question.

"They want to hear the sounds of the jungle," says Silvio.

Malcolm ponders this. "We'll supply them with a tape."

Kip and I volunteer to go along. Rather, Kip volunteers and I go along. Comfortable trips make the worst stories. Best to have something to complain about.

Tonight is Archie's sixty-ninth birthday. Some of us learn for the first time that he was in the CIA from 1947 to 1974 and that he will publish his memoirs this year. Lucky reveals he speaks "about twenty" languages.

After dinner we watch rest of Cousteau documentary, in which Amazonians tell him about pink dolphins seducing women and getting them pregnant.

DAY SIX

We go ashore and hack our way several hundred yards into the jungle to get the flavor of it. After three minutes Malcolm, dripping in sweat, tells Silvio, "I think we've got the point." Hearty agreement all around, but we are urged on by the guides and press on, providing a banquet for ants and mosquitoes.

At lunch Simeon recounts the story of being driven out of Bulgaria by the Communists at age ten, after the Soviets murdered his father, King Boris, and his uncle, the regent. His mother was convinced they were never going to be allowed to leave. When the train carrying him and his mother mysteriously stopped just short of the Turkish border, his mother thought their "Varennes" was at hand: a summary firing squad against the siding. But it was the engineer who had stopped the train, refusing to go any farther. "I will not be the one to drive the

king out of Bulgaria!" It was probably his death warrant. A Turkish engineer was sent for, and Simeon and his mother made it safely out of their country.

Halfway through this much more detailed and spellbinding story, he stops and with no insincerity says, "I think I must be boring you."

We tell him, respectfully, that we will kill him if he doesn't go on. "My God," sputters Malcolm. "Most of us have to read history. We don't get the chance every day to talk to it."

Simeon is a remarkable man: scholarly, pious, a natural raconteur. What a tragedy his country is ruled by thugs. How sad to contemplate the role of the United States in handing Bulgaria over to the Soviets after World War II. "Small countries," he observes, with surprising lack of bitterness, "are traded like currency."

That night I start calling him "Your Majesty." He is amused by this and starts calling me "Your Excellency."

DAY SEVEN

We're about half the way to Iquitos, six hundred miles from Manaus.

Breakfast conversation fixes on the enormous black beetle that has affixed itself to our upper deck during the night. I do not join in the excitement over the errant coleoptera because Kip and I are preparing to helicopter forty-five miles upriver to join up with the *Virginian*s for our night in the jungle.

We land in a soccer field in the town of Fonte Boa, and are swarmed by small children—one of whom I see is wearing a Banana Republic T-shirt—and the king of Greece. Furious preparations are underway aboard *The Virginian* for our expedition. Lord Romsey is packing a Walther PPK, the king has a .38 tucked into his waistband.

Two very hot and unpleasant hours later we are paddling in dugout canoes through the *varzea*, the flooded forest. Piranhas dimple the surface and larger things splash behind half-submerged rubber trees. Vines droop like snakes. The Cutter mosquito repellent—God bless you, Mr. Cutter—burns like acid on our sweat-drenched faces. My admiration for vet-

Some of the Amazonian beasties encountered (we put them all back).

Jungle hackers: MF and guide.

erans of Vietnam, already high, multiplies exponentially.

The king and Lord Romsey go off to shoot deer—or anything furry or feathery that moves. We sit miserably in the dugouts, provender for ectoparasites, chiggers, mosquitoes, and protozoans. (As I write this two weeks later, I scratch at a bubbly rash that has turned my body from head to toe into a Rand McNally relief map.)

After a series of loud shotgun explosions, the king of Greece hoves up in a dugout, looking content and smoking a cigarette. "We had a very nice wander through the forest," he says. "Shot a few trees. One of these fellows," he grins, thumbing back toward the native guides, "was told who I am. He'd never heard of the term. He said to me, 'How do you get to be one of those?' " He laughs. "He said, 'Is it like the ones in the Bible? Why don't you have your crown?' I told him, 'Well, it's a bit hot.' Then he asked me if I knew any pharaohs."

Kip and I end up in a native hut politely but firmly declining the gracious offer of a shared meal of catfish—with head and guts—boiled in Amazon water and poured on manioc.

Hundreds of thousands of fireflies. The guides paddle silently through the forest making a "*Whoaan! Whoaan!*" sound to attract ja-

cares—the Amazonian crocodilians. Enormous insects flit in and out of flashlight beams. Something the size of a bird—but not a bird—lands on my face.

Hours later, back at camp, the king, Pat, and Norton arrive with two small crocs, speared but still alive and looking distinctly pissed off.

We eat a dinner of tomato soup, fruit, and chocolate. Dripping with sweat, reeking, and eyes and cuts stinging with Cutter's, we spend a fitful night in hammocks covered in mosquito netting, listening to the sounds of the guides in the distance hunting jaguar.

DAY EIGHT

A hard rain falls as we paddle back to *The Highlander*, which to these itchy eyes looks like Paris. Breakfast of eggs, bacon, muffins, juice, coffee. It turns out the others went crocodile hunting last night as well. My sense is everyone greatly relieved not to have seen any. While sitting in the back of a dugout, our helicopter pilot, Chuck Dixson, was backed into a termite nest. Chuck is reportedly not in a good mood this morning.

John Kluge arrives to play a few rubbers of bridge. I turn the thermostat to forty below and go to bed between clean sheets. As I drift off I pray to the Lord never to let me take being a middle-class American citizen for granted.

John Kluge is an interesting guy: He made $7,000 playing poker while a scholarship student at Columbia—he was a classmate of Thomas Merton's, whom he remembers as a "playboy." To judge from lunch conversation, he has creamed the *Highlander* crowd at bridge, though he *says* he hasn't played it in fifteen years. Malcolm abdicates his seat to Kip. One must consider before sitting down to cards with the second-wealthiest man in America—the man started with zilch.

That night I start out of my sleep at 3 A.M. when a huge log *thunnngs* into our hull. I walk forward in the hailstorm of insects and stand awhile as the *Highlander*'s searchlight sweeps back and forth across the water. No lights on either shore. *The Virginian* is behind us, slaloming through the logs.

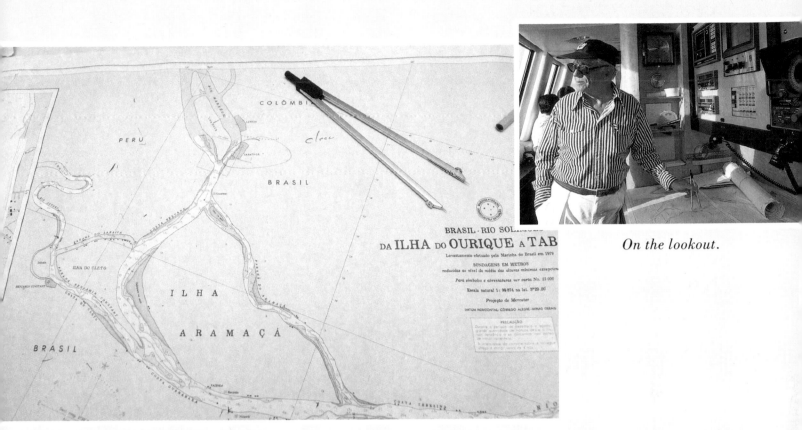

On the lookout.

Into the Heart of Darkness.

A day at the opera.

Day Nine

Nearing Peru now, the river getting narrower, more interesting. Instead of a solid wall of green at river's edge, the jungle opens here and there, revealing emerald pastures and cavernous hollows with liana vines for stalactites. Another new sight: Natives paddle out in their dugouts, waving, to surf in our wake. A strange, but not unwelcome, absence of vultures.

Malcolm announces that the *Virginian*s will be coming over and there will be skeet off the aft deck before lunch. We practice with the twelve-gauge pump guns we have aboard to repel terrorists. Simeon and Margarita, veterans of many Spanish shoots, knock the clay birds down one after another.

Unfortunately, their king and their lord beat our king and our queen. Checkmate.

"The last thing I shot was Germans," grins Malcolm, declining a turn.

Dinner aboard *The Virginian*. The Kluges lay on another fine spread: slices of beef rolled around horseradish cream on fried toast, caviar atop blue cheese, a dripping Brie *en croute*, fresh cakes, and a beautiful split of icy-cold German dessert wine.

Lots of congratulations on having made it through our night in the jungle. "Hold on," I demur, "and see if two months from now we're all covered with scarlet blotches and our noses fall off." (Prescient, that.)

Day Ten

Glenn the steward/bagpiper says he gets up every morning before dawn to practice his bagpiping on the top deck. He says the villagers come down to the water's edge and clap and dance. "It's really something." The crew is, without exception, exceptional.

We visit an Indian village a mile up an estuary, guided by Chuck above in the helo. I crouch in the high-speed Donzi as we make our approach to the village, figuring: Here are two high-speed boats and a helicopter in an area way off the beaten path. If I were the local coke baron, I'd guess I was under attack by a bunch of gringo drug agents disguised as rich WASPs.

But the villagers are welcoming. We exchange gifts and poke around. Everyone wears a little wooden cross around the neck, even the babies.

Later this afternoon we arrive at the junction of Brazil, Colombia, and Peru. As various officials of all three countries amuse themselves with the ship's copier, we go ashore.

Leticia is, you might say, a freebaseport. They assemble untaxed electronics components here, but the city's economy essentially runs on cocaine, brought down from the nearby mountains in paste form, called *pasta basica*. It's sent on from here for further processing into cocaine hydrochloride, the alkaloid that has done so much to improve the quality of life in the United States and elsewhere.

We motor past a flotilla of boats and seaplanes confiscated from drug runners. Carlos, the guide aboard *The Virginian*, keeps up a running monologue as we walk through the streets.

"Over there I watch a man shot. Pow! He have a suitcase with one million dollars. Cash. You see this hotel? The owner killed a few months ago. He wouldn't sell. There on the corner—with the mustache. He was in Manaus three years prison for cocaine. Every day in Leticia—pow!" He shakes his head and frowns.

Their King beats our Queen.

Dad's the power at the bow.

DAY ELEVEN

Getting close, now. The river continuing to narrow; the ship at times steering so close to the bank we can peer deep into the jungle. A curious and not unpleasant sensation, doing that while sitting admidst a Gainsborough and a Toulouse-Lautrec, air-conditioned and sipping Bloody Marys. This is not a Conradian experience.

Sad that tonight is our last—the Captain's Dinner, as the occasion is formally called. We have covered nearly 1,200 miles. Malcolm is an antidote to the horror stories about extreme wealth. He's generous as hell and he likes to have *fun*. A few days earlier Kip told me that Malcolm's father, a dour Scot, had once exploded at his wife, a Catholic girl: "Woman, how can you spend so much money!" "Bertie," she calmly replied, "I *like* spending money."

This afternoon I run into Malcolm. He has the run of the most luxurious yacht afloat, yet there he is—oddly—alone, sitting on the top deck reading a book. We chat as the equatorial sun melts gloriously in an El Greco of blues and oranges. I ask him, well, why the trip? Malcolm looks off into the jungle, probably out of politeness. *What a stupid question!*

"I don't know," he shrugs and smiles.

Despite our magnificent insulation, it has been possible to absorb one or two impressions of Amazonia. What will be memorable ten years from now? Probably that night in the jungle, squatting in the native hut, trying, politely, to fend off a dinner of stewed catfish *dans son jus*. How freely it was given! That and the hard maize was all there was for this large family. If we'd eaten, someone else would not have. I like to think that the spirit of the Amazonians is reducible to that one single act of generosity. An absurd proposition, of course. Shoumatoff writes of watching two Indian boys stoning a dog to death one afternoon out of sheer boredom and wickedness. But we will have our illusions, and the meal in the jungle will remain mine.

As for the river and land, what has surprised me is not the remoteness and the sparseness of the inhabitation, but just the opposite. Given what dire extremes nature has provided—heat, floods, disease, dangers from predators great and microbial—you wonder that man has survived here at all. Even the soil is not the rich land it is popularly supposed—a "counterfeit paradise," in the words of one biologist. That's why, in part, so many Big Thinkers like Daniel Ludwig and Henry Ford have gone bust trying to cultivate it. And why jungle can be turned into permanent desert with the aid of a few bulldozers. Once the web of interlocking fungi beneath the topsoil is disturbed, the verdure turns to moonscape, and remains so.

My own pathetic fallacy would be to say that it has great wit, the Amazon. It outfoxes everyone, from billionaires to bleeding hearts. A few years ago everyone was screaming because it was supposed to be the major source of our oxygen, and the deforestation was said to be tampering with our most basic need, the air we breathe. Now science has determined that our oxygen comes principally from marine algae. The current environmentalist worry is that the extensive deforestation may be playing havoc with the planet's budget of nitrous oxide. The proposition is as wonderful as the river itself: that by plundering the Amazon we are endangering our chief source of laughing gas. I am sanguine. For I know that most laughing gas is manufactured by politicians, not plants.

Malcolm breaks out a Margaux '78 for our last night on the Amazon. After the chocolate sundaes have been piped in, Malcolm is lavishly toasted. Archie reads a poem composed for the occasion. Malcolm toasts his pair of kings—a good hand—and says how ironic it is that the restoration of democracy in their two countries should depend on a restoration of the monarchy. Simeon rises, tears welling, and thanks

him. We are on the verge of sentimentality, so Malcolm stands up, signaling coffee and cigars. "You see," he turns with a wink to the king of Greece, "the advantages of *owning* the boat?"

DAY TWELVE

We arrive at the dock in Iquitos. The current runs at five or six knots, so fast you think you're

still moving. Braided and holstered officials swarm over us, wanting to check our milk. Our Ultra High Temperature *milk*!

We thank, inadequately, the crew for having got us here and pile into cars. The humidity is suffocating; shirts that were crisp five minutes ago are sopping. Only Simeon, dapper in gray suit, seems unwilted. As we pull away I have a last glimpse of King Constantine leaning over the rail of *The Virginian*, a dozen microphones thrust at him, the beautiful Lady Romsey at his side, translating.

Right after takeoff in *The Capitalist Tool*, Malcolm says, "Shall we buzz the ship?" He disappears forward and soon we are on a low run over the harbor. There below is *The Highlander*, looking, for the first time, miniature, like one of the toy boats her owner used to float down the creek by the house he grew up in, dreaming of adventures.

MESSING ABOUT IN BOATS • 95

CHAPTER

3

THE
HIGHWAYMAN

IT'S GREAT
to arrive, but the trip's most
always most of the fun.
From The Savings of Chairman Malcolm

Most dreams, when they're realized, aren't half as dreamy as you dreamt they'd be. But where cars are concerned, my realized dreams have *exceeded* my wildest imaginings.

I grew up at a time when cars were pretty much a be-all and end-all for kids and teenagers. My brothers and I could spot and name every car. I remember the excitement and arguments when Chrysler came out with the Airflow and teardrop design. It turned out to be a bust, but we were impressed by things like that.

And when my father came home with a Pierce-Arrow in 1934, with the headlights coming out of the fenders, we thought that was truly about as good as a car could ever be.

I think for today's young the car has long since ceased to mean everything. Stereos and sound systems, skiing gear and suped-up sneakers are just as or more important. When it comes to wheels, today's teenagers have far more sense than we did. The convertible, complete with rumble seat, was our idea of the acme. Recent generations began the van craze, and what vast sense those made. Fitted out like rolling living rooms, it didn't matter what the weather was. If they were used to wow and

The legendary "Red Bug" from F.A.O. Schwarz: two bucket seats and four wire wheels. My mother and youngest brother, Wally, with Duncan in the driver's seat.

woo, you didn't have to remove seats, or carry blankets, or spend bucks to check in at some remote motel. And they were beautiful—panels, curtains, shag rugs, chrome, the whole bit. I'm not sure that the latest four-wheel preference for high-rise pickup trucks makes as much sense. It's a climb to get in, and who needs a chromed-up roll bar and all those expensive spotlights for a romantic evening? The idea of using those shining, expensive creations to truck something would be considered a blasphemy.

But back to the past, and our four-wheel obsessions.

In 1929 my brothers and I received a fabulous Christmas present—a "Red Bug." From the fabled F.A.O. Schwarz came this platform of slats on four wheels, carrying two bucket seats, in the back of which two car-sized lead batteries were cased. Complete with two foot pedals and a steering wheel, this electric wagon, with its 12-mph capability, was heaven on wheels for us. We were forever fighting over whose turn it was to tool around the neighborhood until the batteries died, which they did every couple of hours.

My fascination with cars has yet to run down. Today the super ones, the extraordinary ones, the exotic ones, are the biggest turn-on. Most of our current cars are practical, functional. People get into them to go where they're going, but if you have the bread, and the ultimate exotics make the adrenaline run, getting in to go anywhere is a trip. The car

PREVIOUS SPREAD: *Lamborghini 5000 Quattrovalvole, the Countach.*

that I use around New York is one that I first saw when in Munich on our balloon/motorcycle Friendship Tour through Germany. As we were leaving the hotel to bike up and away, a fabulous, sleek four door sedan purred up. It turned out to be an Aston Martin Lagonda. For most people, a bell rings when they see an Aston Martin, because it often has a co-starring role in James Bond epics. It was a while before I

the phone. But when I get into the Lamborghini, I want to drive. It's the ultimate jewel.

In addition to a Countach being itself an art form, getting into one is also something of an art. You really have to learn how to get in and out, because once in, you're practically sitting on the ground. And there are other disadvantages. The rearview-mirror vision is pretty limited, and it's no car to be taking the family away

Aston Martin Lagonda, the twin of James Bond's favorite get-away car, in front of the Town House at 11 West 12th Street, adjacent to the Forbes *Building.*

had one by the wheel, because Aston Martin makes fewer than two hundred a year and they are spoken for before they come out, painstakingly handcrafted, from the factory. The other sublime car we have is Lamborghini's Countach, an absolute piece of sculpture. It surely belongs someplace like the Museum of Modern Art, as it represents the apex in styling to date that I know of, a production car that derives from a racing car. In the Piedmontese dialect, "Countach" means "fantastic verging on incredible," and that just about says it.

The Countach loves turns. It waits for them, relishes them. It wants you to "put the pedal to the metal" when you round a corner. It eats up corners. I'm driven a lot, and that's basically what the Lagonda is for: I sit and read and use

for the weekend in because it only holds two. If you're going to the grocery store with it, you'll have to shop alone, because a bag of groceries will completely fill the next seat. Too, you can't sit in it with your top hat on. But I'd rather leave the topper at home or take a motorcycle to the opera. And then there are the toll booths. Because the windows are so low and curved, they only open about two inches, so you have to flip up the door to pay the toll. Things like that.

Still, it's the kind of car that everybody loves to look at. It doesn't engender the kind of resentment that stretch limos do, with all that dark glass—the pretentious hallmark that says to the world, "Look at me, I have this enormously expensive car." Those things are a turnoff. I don't want to be in one until I'm dead.

Nobody gets mad when they see the Countach. When I stop at a traffic light, everybody, whether on a bicycle, in rags or splendid attire, or just hurrying home—everybody whistles and smiles and signals thumbs up. Two times out of three, people roll down their window and ask, "What kind of car is that?" Unfortunately, I can't roll mine down in return.

Something like the Countach is disarming, I think, because people can imagine the enthusiasm that went into its acquisition. Buying one would be the ultimate car trip. So, instead of saying, "Oh, look at that son-of-a-bitch, showing off the money he's got," they probably think, "God, if I had the money, I'd do that, too." It's the "Wow!" factor.

Our third set of wheels is the most mindboggling: the Lamborghini Jeep. Huge, with abrupt styling, it looks like a Space Age version of a Rommel World War II command car. Driven by the same massive 12-cylinder power pack as the Countach, with its wide wide tires

Lamborghini Jeep—roughing it, Italian style. A Desert-Fox chassis, but underneath purrs the same classy power plant as the Countach.

it can go 131 mph across desert sand, which virtue is of limited use in New Jersey. Nor is there much use for it in the Big Apple. Anyway, just to lift up that hood and look at the maze of electronics and engine and pipes and wires is a turn-on.

And given the fact that the city is a minefield of potholes, this stark quasi-tank rides with the comfort of a Cadillac. Extraordinary to see, fabulous to drive. My grandchildren are thrilled and impressed whenever I pick them up in it. So am I.

As for antique cars, like everyone I love to see them, but I don't have the dedication and passenger Packard sedan, amply able to hold our parents and the five of us. It was a memorably splendid car, so when I heard about a painstakingly restored 1932 Packard touring car that was for sale, I was instantly turned on. 1932 was really almost the end of the line for great Packards. We were in the depth of the Depression, and great luxury cars weren't moving. To try to survive, the company introduced the Packard 120, a little version of the big old Packard. Unfortunately, it didn't succeed in saving the company.

I fell instantly in love with the restored '32 tourer. It had been meticulously brought back

The Lamborghini Countach—flaps up and ready for take-off. Its minimalist windows mean flipping up the driver's wing for turnpike toll-paying.

Lamborghini jewel box.

devotion it takes to be a connoisseur or collector of them. Some years back I couldn't resist a 1909 Renault, and with the kids piled in we would use it once in a while to chug over to the neighbors', but, more often than not, one difficulty or another would make completing the trip a challenge which I was not able to meet.

Our current oldie goldie is a 1932 Twin Six Packard touring car. Packard's slogan, "Ask the man who owns one," was one of the most memorable and long-lasting in the history of automobile advertising. In the twenties and thirties Packard ranked high among the best cars in America. We had a brown 1929 seven-

to the way it looked when it was new, with the folding rear-seat windshield for the people in the back; the distinctive radiator grill, as well known in its day as that of the Rolls Royce; the headlamps, like those of the Pierce-Arrow, coming out of the fenders; the heavy, vaultlike doors: all the solid details that spoke of an era that was pre-plastic, pre-electronic, pre-recall.

What's more, that grand old car was the product of an enormously competitive era. There were some two hundred car-makers up until the Depression, and almost all of them disappeared in that long, dark economic night. Very few survived, but it was a time that, in retrospect, was marked by top quality, reliability, dealer integrity and functional design. To me, that car epitomized the absolute best of those old values.

The '32 Twin Six was delivered at home on a trailer, and I think the restorer, who had spent months lovingly going over every inch, was a little taken aback that I planned to drive it on real roads. Our maiden voyage started out in high style. We were on our way to Morristown, and I felt like a kid again. Then, as we came to a stoplight, the brakes seemed to be giving way. I had to stop with the hand brake. The engine died and wouldn't restart. We had to get out and ignominiously push my perfect antique

Packard to the side of the road.

Things have gone better since. We've learned to cope with its idiosyncrasies. I use it with my kids and grandchildren, and feel only a little phony driving it because I didn't myself pour all that love and affection into the arduous restoration. I just bought it.

I wasn't exposed to the joys of motorcycling until I was forty-eight years old, and I have been trying to make up for lost time ever since. A man who worked for me wanted to borrow money to buy a motorcycle, and I told him I didn't want to lend him the money to kill himself. I had the usual attitude of the uninitiated toward motorcycles. He convinced me it was *his* life and only my money. He bought a gleaming new 1967 Triumph and gave me a ride on the back, and I got a terrific kick out of the experience.

So, the next week I went out and bought a little 90cc. Now, to all the rest of the world a 90cc. is a small bike. It was a Honda, and they called it a trailbike. Which fit in perfectly, because we had a lot of horse trails around home, and I would pick times when the horses were totally out of the picture and have great fun driving my new trailbike. In fact, I had so much fun that two weeks later I went back and bought

1932 Twin Six Packard touring car; a vintage pre-war machine, pre-plastic and pre-recall.

The Forbes 10-year retail experiment, our motorcycle shop in Whippany, New Jersey. Of course, customers came first in service, and the owner had to wait—so I sold it in 1979—lock, stock and cylinders. Now that I'm back to being a good customer, service is terrific.

a street bike, and that began my real love affair with motorcycles.

As a result, two of my sons wanted motorcycles for graduation, and I ended up buying so many at retail that I thought it would be cheaper to buy them wholesale, so I bought the shop I had been dealing with and moved it to a new location. Soon we were doing over $2 million worth of sales a year in motorcycles old and new, plus gear and spare parts—a big thriving motorcycle emporium right there in Whippany, New Jersey.

I kept it for ten years, during which time I discovered the Syndrome of the Shoemaker's Kids. We were always trying to put the customer first, because he was paying and I wasn't, so I never got the priority that I'd had when I was a customer at the shop—a good customer. So I sold it, and went back to being a good customer and the joy of priority that thereunto pertains.

When I started riding, I'd had to face up to the fear of trying something new. If you've never ridden a horse, you're petrified of the whole idea, but then you do it and you discover by saddle is a wonderful way to go. But you don't discover that until you try it.

When you're a youngster and some of your friends have gone away with their families in the winter and learned how to ski, and you haven't, then you're afraid to try it for fear you'll look foolish. So you say you don't like it, and you build up an aggressive negative. You just can't bring yourself to say, "Gee, I'm afraid of looking foolish."

And then you get to be a little long in life and it seems too late to take something up. And eventually it *is* too late.

I think of things that it really is too late for me to do now. Hang-gliding, for instance. I would have been into hang-gliding ten years ago, if it's only half as much fun as it looks. But I didn't. And parachute jumping. And skiing. I liked everything about skiing, but I never got around to doing it, and I wish I had. Now I would be too uncoordinated, I'm afraid, and possibly a little brittle-boned. But I still wish I had.

The appeal of motorcycling is hard to explain to someone who has never done it. To those many who have questioned me about the sanity of what rapidly became a real passion for two-wheelers, I have often and patiently pointed out that on a motorcycle you can't be unaware of the environment, you integrate with it. You feel the temperature change from mountain to valley. You smell the crops in the fields. You're alert to what's going on around you because motorcyclists who do not stay alert tend to have very short careers.

Tooling around on a motorcycle, you have a sense of independence that must be somewhat akin to the way the cowpokes of the Old West felt when they mounted their horses. You feel an awareness, if not always a oneness, with the elements. You totally relate to nature and the environment. If there are dark clouds ahead, are you apt to be caught by rain? Should you stop and suit up for it? If the early morning and the night are going to be cold, how cold? How many layers of clothing?

And speaking of clothing, it's helpful if people understand about bikers and leather. Leather happens to be the strongest material practical for motorcycling clothing—it's the only armor between you and ripped skin in case of a fall. In spite of their bad image, leathers indicate total good sense. If you see someone on a motorcycle in cutoffs, T-shirt and sneakers, then you can properly conclude not that they're crazy for riding a motorcycle, but that they're crazy for not respecting the motorcycle. To the rest of the world, you should be less suspect in leathers than if you were wearing cutoffs.

Incidentally, the superiority of leather may not hold forever. I have a set of Kevlar-lined denims made by a company that tried to make a go of it in motorcycling clothing about ten years ago. Kevlar, of course, is stronger than steel, but by the time you build it into a suitable lining it's pretty bulky. I gave one of the jackets to President Reagan after the shooting attempt on his life, suggesting that he might make us all feel safer if he wore it for horseback riding and wood chopping. Anyway, if the problem of making Kevlar lining more supple can be solved, there's a future for this type of garment somewhere down the road.

As for helmets, maybe riders should have the option of wearing 'em, but I think it's mighty foolish not to. I would be dead now as a result of the accident I had in Montana's Glacier National Park a while back had I not been wearing a helmet. I recovered from the concussion, the collapsed lung and the three broken ribs quickly—in just ten days I felt up to a balloon ride—but without the helmet it might have been my last ride.

The "Capitalist Tools" rev up for a Sunday "poker run" at Timberfield.

I keep two Harley Springer motorcycles in the basement garage of my New York headquarters. When I first started riding a motorcycle around Manhattan, I'd stop in front of the Waldorf or "21" for a business lunch and the doormen would get angry and tell me I couldn't leave it in front. Most of them recognize me now, because I'm often a customer of what's behind the doors and curbs over which they reign. Some have to be reminded that these street curbs are public property. No motorcyclist has to let himself be run off by these sometimes overpossessive, overdressed portal commanders.

Motorcyclists also seem to irritate a lot of motorists. Some motorists unfortunately do more than irritate motorcyclists. They often bang them up or kill 'em. Usually not deliberately. One reason they don't like us is because it's irksome if your car is piled up in a couple of lanes of solid traffic at a light and somebody on a bike passes easily between the lanes to the front of the line you're fuming about.

Strictly speaking, I'm not a collector of motorcycles, I simply have a lot of them. It's one area where "old" is not what I'm into. If I have a motorcycle more than three or four years old, it's only because the maker hasn't come out with anything better. With bikes I'm in favor of the newest and the best, and I keep a garage full of the latest and the hottest.

There are about forty-five bikes in the garage at Timberfield, my home in New Jersey, two that stay on the *Highlander*, four or five in London and four, I think, in Morocco. And then there are a number of dirt bikes out at Trinchera, the ranch in Colorado, as well as half-a-dozen tour bikes which we keep there for our summer Western trips.

The variety of machinery at these locations runs the full gamut of motorcycling's many choices. We've got the fully loaded touring mounts—Honda's Gold Wing and Yamaha's Venture most notable among the long-distance specialists—and a mouth-watering array of Harley-Davidson's finest. There are the pure sport bikes, including two Italian-built Bimotas, sport tourers personified by BMW R- and K-series cycles, and even outrageous hot rods like the Yamaha V-Max. I've also acquired a number of very limited-production machines: a pair of Kawasaki-based Vetter Mystery Ships, an Amazonas from Brazil and a Münch from Germany. There is also a pair of British Heskeths and a sprinkling of old favorites, such as the Soviet bike we picked up on our tour of Russia.

Often I am asked what's my favorite motorcycle, and it's not hard to name the favorite brand: Harley-Davidson. They're just unduplicatable. The Japanese have made many supe-

Black tied MF arriving for a private dinner honoring Nancy Reagan during Mikhail Gorbachev's 1988 visit to New York City. On a bike it was easy to bypass Gorby-locked limos.

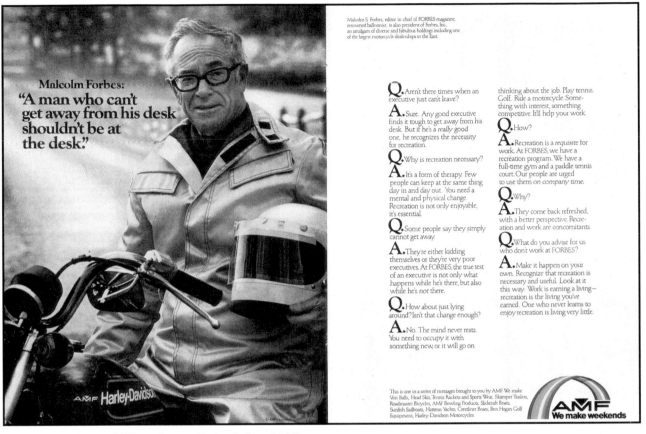

Saddle-wisdom, MF-style, solicited by AMF, who owned Harley-Davidson at the time.

rior Japanese Harley look-alikes, but they make them too well. They hum like sewing machines. The gearshift is noiseless. On a Harley you *know* you've shifted gears. You can hear the throatiness of your engine. And the Japanese have never been able to make a seat as comfortable as Harley has.

More than a simple matter of conspicuous purchasing, the motorcycle supply of the Forbes fleet is just a way of saying that I don't want to ever have to be without one to ride. Sometimes it's just for pleasure with friends; other times the tours are a break from the business of Forbes Inc. And there are the Friendship Tours, which marry two of my deepest devotions, cycling and hot-air ballooning, to promote friendship and understanding between the United States and our global neighbors.

Motorcycles are like racehorses. You want to have the best bloodlines, and that means to have a Harley, if you can. It's the most sought-after motorcycle in the world, not just here but in Japan, Europe, all around the globe.

Once when we were on our way to Norway's North Cape, up above the Arctic Circle, I crashed one of our bikes and we found three guys in this little snowbound village who had pooled their money and built a Harley Rat from parts they could find. They were great mechanics and had the Tour Glide ready to roll the next day. It's like that all over the world. People are attracted to motorcycles because of the freedom and freewheeling spirit they represent. If they know anything about bikes, they especially love Harleys.

Sometimes people ask me what I think about "real" bikers—presumably guys with dirty fingernails and thick beards who fix their own machines and don't change their clothes for a week.

Actually, in the beginning I felt the same way that most—too many—still feel about motorcycles: that they're highly dangerous and that the people on them must be a little nuts. Either thrill-seekers, quirky or at least very odd.

Huge Münch TTS motorcycle from Germany, hand-crafted by Friedel Münch with a 1200 c.c. NSU automobile engine.

Two Bimota motorcycles, custom-made road racing machines. The chrome moly steel chassis are Italian, with re-worked Suzuki engines.

Russian-made 125 c.c. Voskhod-2 bike, an unsuccessful Soviet export over a decade ago that never really took off.

That's basically the attitude in this country, and it was certainly the one I had, because where I grew up nobody in the local schools ever had a motorcycle. And when you saw them, the fellows on them had leather helmets and goggles. They were esoteric and apart from the lives of most people.

Originally in this country, motorcycles were essentially sport machines. They had a certain romance to them, and it was only later that they

Lord Hesketh's attempt to revive the British bike industry failed. Here, the V-1000 c.c. sport model.

Amazonas bike (Brazil). Adapting a regular Volkswagen engine to two wheels, it was one of the only motorcycles in the world with a reverse gear until the 1989 Honda Aspencade appeared.

THIS FXRS MADE THE
FIRST FOREIGN MOTORCYCLE TRIP
THROUGH
THE PEOPLE'S REPUBLIC OF CHINA
IN OCTOBER 1982
ALSO THROUGH PAKISTAN
IN APRIL 1983
AND THROUGH EGYPT
IN FEBRUARY/MARCH 1984

Interior of the motorcycle garage at Timberfield, haven for veteran bikes and awards repository. The bike on the wall, a 1982 1340 c.c. Harley FXRS, was retired with full honors after surviving the China, Pakistan and Egypt Friendship Tours.

came to stand for the one percent who fostered the image of black leather and sleaze that is associated with bikers and their bikes today. In Europe there is a whole different outlook, and motorcycling has always been much more acceptable. But here motorcycles weren't all that widespread through the twenties and thirties, appealing mostly to daredevils who, for one reason or another, didn't go into race-car driving. But then, beginning in the forties, cycling seemed to acquire a rough reputation. It started to take on a culture of its own, involving beer, beards and bellies. And I must admit I shared much of that point of view about bikes until I got into it.

Part of the problem may be that a lot of business types haven't grown up exposed to biking, but that's changing, too. My son Tim, who's a cycling enthusiast, and a couple of our advertising people have discovered that quite a number of the younger but key people in the advertising world love to motorcycle.

Most motorcyclists I know cherish the freedom simply to get on their bike and go, yet at the same time they love to meet others who share the feeling that motorcycles don't just symbolize freedom, they induce it.

I think, unquestionably, that the Capitalist Tools have helped motorcyclists' image. The Tools are the Forbes road pack: friends, acquaintances, business execs, political types, show-business luminaries, journalists, motorcycle reps—they've all Capitalist Tooled with us. Of those who ride with me, often as many as half are people who work for *Forbes* and share the same interest. It's not a job requisite; they just get bitten by the bug.

Part of what's distinctive about the Capitalist Tools is that everybody wears a red-and-gold Capitalist Tool vest. On the highway we get the most incredulous stares when people spot the logo on our back and it says "Capitalist Tools" instead of something more sinister-sounding. Some motorists and bikers ask us what kind of tools we make. And I explain that our tool takes the form of a magazine that tries to tune up the performance of corporations.

Our weekend "poker runs" are yet another reason that people may be coming around in their thinking. From May to October, as often as I'm home, I go on as many as I can. A local motorcycle club will play host and lay out a predetermined route which we all follow. We rendezvous at a clubhouse, usually a motorcycle shop, for coffee and doughnuts, and then for the next two hours or so we follow the coded directions that show the way—directions that most motorists would miss altogether. For example, if you see a splat "dot" of lime in the road, that might mean "Straight ahead at the next intersection." Two such say "Left turn coming up." Three, a right turn. Three wavy lines stand for "Dangerous piece of road ahead" —a one-lane bridge, perhaps.

Along the way we'll come to a place where we'll all pull in and each rider draws a card from a pack. At the end of the run, whoever drew the highest card wins the pot, made up from part of the admission charge for the run. And then there's food, drawings for biking gear, the chance to kick tires and examine the newest and the oldest, lie a lot and check each other's cycle out.

We almost invariably get the trophy for being the most-represented group, an honor that's unrelated to any special on-the-road skills. We're just good at getting lots of people to join us in enjoying the event.

And then some Sundays I may be asked to be the grand marshal for a charity ride sponsored by the Cancer Society or maybe Muscular Dystrophy. We usually take along the purple Harley I gave to Elizabeth Taylor (purple for her Passion perfume, and for her eyes), because people enjoy seeing that if they can't see Elizabeth, and five or six of us will fly to the site on the Forbes plane, also named the *Capitalist Tool*, participate in the run and fly back the same day.

It's a slow erosion, but it's happening: people are realizing that not everybody on a motorcycle is a gangster, a drug dealer or a nut. I suppose I've come to represent motorcycling to a lot of people who've never been on a bike, but others may be thinking it's just another example of how age and presumed intelligence didn't necessarily come together in my case.

MF makes one thing perfectly clear as he and co-enthusiast Elizabeth Taylor model the distinctive biker rings they purchased for one another.

The Passion purple Sportster Harley-Davidson (above, left), decorated by Willie Davidson person-ally, that MF presented to Elizabeth Taylor. The violet fuel tank faithfully mirrors E.T.'s volatile eyes, as well as her Passion perfume packages.

Two for the road.

The appeal of motorcycling is hard to explain to someone who's never done it. It's not the risk that makes the adrenaline run. It's in the biking. The zest for the road on two wheels. You appreciate when the sun comes out after it's been raining. When I'm in a car, I never see a motorcyclist go by without thinking about what he or she is riding. And when I'll be on a motorcycle again.

Then there's the danger factor. Sure, motorcycling has risks. If you're hit, it's more likely to hurt than if you're sealed up in a car. But you know that, so all your senses are more alert. People fall asleep in cars, but did you ever hear of anybody falling asleep on a bike?

A couple of bad falls have introduced me to doctors I never would have met but for motorcycling, but I've never thought for a minute about giving it up. You can't go through life insulating yourself from danger. Everything is dangerous. Living is dangerous. Eventually, everybody dies of it.

THE HIGHWAYMAN • 111

King Hassan II of Morocco receives a two-wheeled mount from MF for the royal stable in 1972. To the horror of His Majesty's security-conscious retinue, the delighted Hassan promptly piloted his new steed, Steve McQueen-style, straight out through the palace gates.

Two-Wheeling Through America's West

IN 1987, *MOTORCYCLE* MAGAZINE EDITOR ART FRIEDMAN REPORTS:

THE ROAD GLIDES beneath you. The sky flows over you. The wind rushes past, bringing new sounds and smells. Uninsulated, you touch the world as you press through it unencumbered by a cage. Beneath you, the machine hums and throbs, almost alive. It blends with you, telling you of the road surface and responding to your every movement.

There is a world waiting out there along America's highways, but you'll hardly touch it in a car, encased in steel and glass. The best way to discover it is from the saddle of a motor-cycle, where you can feel, hear and smell your environment from a seat with horizon-to-horizon visibility.

The best motorcycle touring in the world may be found in the American West. At least, that is the informed opinion of Malcolm Forbes, who has ridden through dozens of countries with his fleet of motorcycles. Although his annual Friendship Tours, which combine business, diplomacy and the pleasures of motorcycling and ballooning in other nations, have captured the world's attention, Forbes and his Capitalist

En route in Utah, posing for Vanity Fair's *1987 "Hall of Fame."*

Tool riding companions actually have more pure fun and have covered thousands more miles on the highways of North America.

Forbes' western headquarters at the 400-square-mile Forbes Trinchera Ranch in southern Colorado is ideally situated for forays through the Rockies, the southwestern deserts and the West Coast. For his eleventh such foray in as many years, the destination was Sturgis, S.D., where 50,000 to 60,000 motorcyclists congregate each year to socialize and ride through the Black Hills. Instead of setting out northeast toward the hills, the Capitalist Tools head west from the ranch toward Utah.

Only scattered clouds dot the sky as the Capitalist Tools' road show falls into line. Soon we are cascading down a series of switchbacks, racing the water from melting snow down into mountain valleys. Ahead rain clouds build up. Soon a thunderstorm is beating up a butte off to our right. When we finally reach the storm, Forbes never stops.

"I keep believing it will stop just ahead," he explains. "And by the time I realize that it's not going to, we're already as wet as we're going to get." As if the gods of weather recognize political boundaries, the sky clears immediately as we ride into Utah.

The next morning, we have an 80-mile ride to meet photographer Annie Leibovitz, who is photographing Forbes for *Vanity Fair* (see back cover). The setting is a canyon alongside the Colorado River, with Forbes and his Harley set against the red rock bluffs. While Chairman Malcolm roasts in his leathers beneath the climbing sun, the rest of us watch. Eventually, the image is captured and the Capitalist Tools set loose again.

We are traveling on U.S. 6 in Utah, which is not an interstate highway, so the speed limit is still 55. However, we are all pretty impatient and soon we are over 70 mph, swinging around the slower traffic on a 20-mile upgrade. Utah's state troopers have a reputation for diligence, and when my Passport radar detector beeps for just an instant, every cop sensor in my body is alert. Forbes pulls ahead of the rest of us, who have gotten brief electronic warnings. There are no oncoming radar cars or roadside speed traps, and everybody is beginning to think it's a false alarm when a white Turbo Mustang charges up behind us, blasts past and pulls Forbes over at the crest. The rest of us follow.

What results is a traffic nightmare. None of the licenses are from Utah and three of them are from out of the country. All eight bikes have Colorado license plates with "MSF" and a single digit—and all are insured through New Jersey. Nonetheless, the constable is diligently prepared to write up the whole lot of us, despite Forbes' willingness to take the blame. ("They are all on my bikes and they were following me.") Then the officer's captain shows up, tells him what a great job he's doing and that we all deserve it. *That* seems to change the officer's attitude. Only Forbes gets a ticket; the rest of us get written warnings.

'88 *Western Trip (L-R): Stephane Lair, Nick Ienatsch, Dr. Jan Engzelius, MF, Uwe Schwarzwalder.*

The fourth day's leg brings the breathtaking vistas of Grand Teton and Yellowstone National Parks. In the process, we discover that it is easier to pass bison on a motorcycle than in a motor home. We arrive at the evening's destination, Forbes' Mountain House near Gardiner, Montana. After a 25-minute Jeep ride up a dirt access road, we find ourselves literally on top of the world. From this house hanging on the edge of a mountaintop, you can see perhaps 50 miles up the Yellowstone Valley, and civilization is a long way away. As if to confirm that, Errol Ryland, manager of Trinchera Ranch and a former game biologist, warns us: "There are grizzlies up here. If you see a bear, make lots of noise and walk—don't run—in the opposite direction."

At Mount Rushmore, television crews await us. The Sturgis Motorcycle Classic is an important local event. In Sturgis, every inch of the main street is lined with motorcycles parked handlebar to handlebar at the curb and down the center of the street. The constant question is about when the huge balloon in the shape of a Harley-Davidson bike will fly.

By 8 p.m. a suitable launch site protected from the wind has been found. The balloon rises into the sunset-painted sky on its first free flight in America. A slight breeze catches it, blowing it directly over and along the main street. Below, tens of thousands of motorcyclists raise their voices in a roar of approval that for a minute drowns out the rumble of engines.

(L-R): MF, Jan, and Utah trooper. Instant radar foils our fuzz-busters.

SUMMER SUNSHINE BRINGS the mountains alive, melting the heavy snows of winter and uncovering all but the highest elevations. A Rocky Mountain summer also brings Malcolm Forbes and a small group of motorcyclists with a 12-year tradition of touring the Rocky Mountains and the West. The 1988 version of this tour meanders from Fort Garland, Colorado, to Los Angeles by the most circuitous route possible.

From western Colorado we meander into southern Utah. Our pace slows as the riders gape at the constantly changing scenery unrolling around us. Bryce Canyon, one of the smallest national parks in Utah, isn't really a canyon at all. Weather and rock have combined to produce rock sculptures on the edge of a plateau, and much of the park is actually tableland. With its intricate yet powerful display of erosion, Bryce appears magically alien, a timeless wonder that only time could create. The fingers of rock in Spires of the Silent City, Queens Garden or at the Wall of Windows appear bizarre, forms from another planet. Our group stops at Bryce Natural Bridge just past sunrise. None of us will forget the changing colors of the rock as the sun rose above us to start our day of traveling.

While Bryce Canyon charms its visitors with panoramic views of enormous delicacies, Zion

Looking Buffaloed!

National Park hits with the subtlety of Mike Tyson. Red rocks reach to the heavens, surrounding and imprisoning the traveler in a canyon cut by the Virgin River and its tributaries. Standing alone at any spot is a humbling experience because of the soaring cliffs and skyscrapers of red rock. We wheel over the red pavement made from the surrounding rock through the Zion-Mt. Carmel Tunnel. Opened in 1930, six galleries in the 1.1-mile-long tunnel let in light and give the traveler an awesome view of the surrounding canyon walls from about 4,800 feet. Staring up at the man-made windows cut in the rock after exiting the tunnel, we appreciate the natural ruggedness of the cliff, yet wonder at the audacity of the men who cut the tunnel and formed the galleries.

Waking up in Bryce Canyon and falling asleep in Las Vegas runs the gamut of the West and can be done in one day of traveling. Vegas squats in the desert of southern Nevada, radiating heat, neon and concrete. The time spent in front of the Palace is typical for Malcolm Forbes. He always seems to have time for people. Kids stop him in his tracks and reduce his vocabulary to babbling kiddy talk. A friendly youngster will find himself fussed over and whispered to. I've seen it happen all over the world, with his granddaughter in New Jersey and a preschooler in Japan. Though Forbes receives a lot of attention wherever he goes, he returns that attention in a very personal way.

As quickly as our group poured out of Utah, we are off again. After the hot flatness of Highway 95, the cool mountain passes of California refresh and reinvigorate us. Highway 168 is The Perfect Road—a civil engineer's imagination run wild, a roller-coaster road with rights and lefts sweeping up and down the terrain. No centerline and a bit of gravel here and there keep us interested when the road isn't winding down the center of a creek bed or doubling back on itself like a snake coming down a circular staircase.

The next morning we enter the east side of

Yosemite National Park on the Tioga Pass. I stand in awe of Yosemite, wary of writing anything at all about the park in fear that I won't stop writing until it is described in the minutest detail. Yosemite is granite cliffs towering half a mile over the valley floor. Yosemite is the giant sequoia trees that grow only on the western slope of California's Sierra Nevadas; they are the world's largest living beings. Yosemite is the mysterious Half Dome, the granite dome cleaved neatly in half by weather, ice and the earth's shifts. Yosemite is nature in full form, featuring black bears, lightning storms, wild flowers and four distinct seasons.

Leaving Yosemite gives me a feeling the tour is practically over, the sights are seen and it's on to civilized, overpopulated California. Nothing about the ride into San Francisco changes this opinion as we struggle through traffic in Oakland and all across the Oakland Bay Bridge into the heart of 'Frisco. My slight depression over leaving the Wild West behind lasts until we hit California's Highway 1, or Pacific Coast Highway. The openness of the ocean provides the same get-away-from-it-all feeling the mountains of Utah do.

Coast Highway connects California's two most populous areas, the bay area of San Francisco and Los Angeles, yet the strip of about 75 miles between Monterey and San Luis Obispo hasn't felt the encroachment of man to any large degree. The smooth coast road couldn't be better the day we follow it in and around the picturesque bays and rocky outcrops of the Pacific Ocean's eastern edge. The road follows the shoreline closely, giving the traveler an eyeful of unlimited horizons as the sea stretches to meet the sky.

We stick to the coast as long as possible. Then through Malibu to Sunset Boulevard. Our group comes out of the wilds to the full glory of California civilization. The 1988 tour officially ends as Malcolm Forbes steps out of his hotel room and up to the lights of the news camera and the microphone of an interviewer.

"Where are we?" (L-R): Errol Ryland, MF, Nick Ienatsch.

High noon at Ranch Headquarters. (L-R): MF, Trinchera manager Errol Ryland, photographer Glen Davis, Scotsman David Patterson, France's Christophe Adde, Norway's Dr. Jan Engzelius, Brett Broege, Motorcyclist editor Art Friedman.

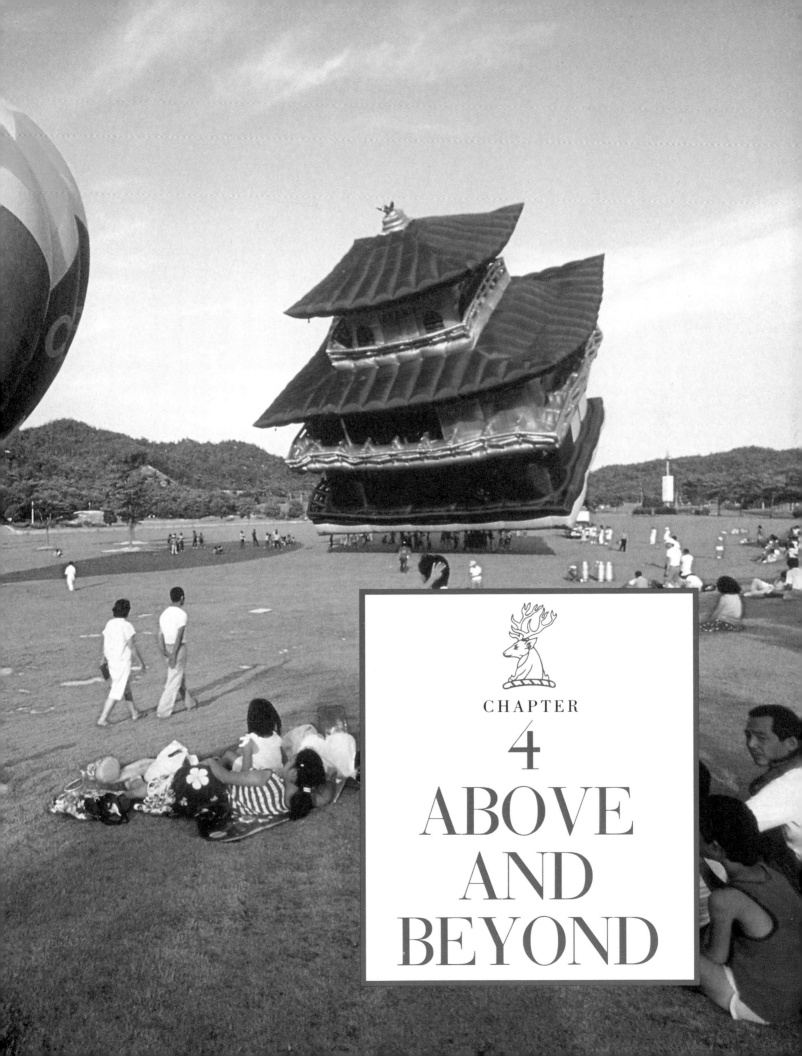

CHAPTER

4

ABOVE
AND
BEYOND

Bᴀᴄᴋ ɪɴ ᴛʜᴇ ᴅᴀʏs of Pullman cars when traveling, I used to fall asleep to the sound of the rails. Now I sleep like a top to the sound of jet engines.

The *Capitalist Tool*, our money-green-and-gold Boeing 727, is the biggest member of the Forbes air force, and it is the third large plane to carry the name. In addition to the big *Tool*, we have a more diminutive version, a Piper Navajo Chieftain named the *Capitalist Tool Too*, that serves guests on Laucala, our island in the Fijis; a Bell 206 JetRanger helicopter, the *Highland Fling*, that roosts on the *Highlander*; and an Agusta helicopter, based in Newark, which we use for megalopolis travel—Philadelphia, Boston, Washington, etc.

Our first plane was a Convair 590 propjet, and we acquired it some twenty years ago. It had a long-range capability and lots of space. We purchased it, essentially, because as a company we were "going global" in the 1970s. We had acquired properties in the South Pacific, England, France and, for an Arabic edition of the magazine, Morocco. We also began to develop substantial real-estate holdings in Colorado, Montana and Wyoming that involved a great deal of travel into towns where sched-uled service was rare.

It was succeeded by a DC-9, and then, after a couple of years' hiatus, we were able to pick up our present Boeing 727 *Tool* at a reasonable price (everything being relative) from Braniff, which, unfortunately, was folding at the time.

We planned to do the interior in the conventional executive configuration similar to that of our previous planes. But Jon Bannenberg, the designer of the latest *Highlander*, who had never done a plane before, asked if he could have a try at a different interior layout. All of us were so impressed with what he had created for the *Highlander* that we were delighted to let him do it. What he came up with is the most stunning airliner insides I have ever seen. It's a quiet knockout.

The plane seats twenty-two, with a crew of four. The chairs and the sofas can be set up so that nine people can sleep fully stretched out and not in reclining chairs. With the number of times the *Tool* is in the Pacific and in Europe, that sleeping capacity is often fully utilized.

Whenever we land, heads never fail to swivel when they see FORBES CAPITALIST TOOL illuminated in can't-miss capital letters on the tail. In most instances it amuses/bemuses those who see it on the runways and in the airports. As a matter of policy, we never hangar the *Tool*. Better it should sit out on the tarmac and beam its message. Much of what I do is done to promote our business and enjoy life (but not necessarily in that order). At *Forbes* we are not engaged in an enterprise where anonymity is a virtue, and our corporate aircraft serves as a flying billboard. For *Forbes* it's the equivalent of what the blimp is for Goodyear.

MF hanging around in the lobby as well as every place else (by Claudio Bravo).

120 • MORE THAN I DREAMED

When we first utilized "Capitalist Tool" in our advertising some twenty-five years ago, the word "capitalist" had been expropriated by the Left and the Reds as an accusatory put-down. It was usually coupled with "pig." For many, the word conjured up visions of somebody with a top hat and a great potbelly, smoking a cigar while sitting on moneybags and squeezing the lifeblood out of hapless peons. "Capitalist" was supposed to be something you either apologized

The biggest menace to free enterprise is not its critics, but those who fail at it. It's the guy who doesn't make a profit who is the villain of the free system. Nothing confirms freedom like a buck in the bank.

We very seldom get a negative reaction to the "Capitalist Tool" name, and we're usually able to make our point. People know I'm not an apologist for the capitalist system. I'm a determined advocate as well as a visible beneficiary of it.

The Capitalist Tool *Boeing 727-100; Agusta 109-A Helicopter; Bell 206 JetRanger* Highland Fling, *based on the* Highlander.

for or denied you were. I think that by virtue of a good-humored twist describing the magazine and naming our planes *Capitalist Tool* we hit upon a jocular way to rehabilitate an abused word and restore its original meaning. Capitalism is nothing more or less than freedom of enterprise and the incentive system—the right of anybody to take a little money and start a business; to make a bundle if the venture succeeds or lose one's shirt if it fails.

How the wheel has turned in relation to capitalism. Many who used to be capitalism's leading detractors, the militant proponents of Communism and revolution, are now busting their picks to install a capitalistic economic framework of their own. They've seen that the motivation for individuals to keep some of what they earn, in an entrepreneurial spirit, is what gives the dynamic quality to the economies of the strong and free nations. They have realized that political decisions which impact an economy are no substitute for a true economy where competition is both spark and fuel.

Fiji based twin-engine Piper Chieftain, Capitalist Tool Too.

From jet prop Convair 580 . . .

. . . to McDonnell Douglas DC9-15 . . .

Inside the fuselage a Jon Bannenberg creation.

. . . to today's Boeing 727.

"The only thing I can actually fly is hot air—in balloons."

N605FM (standing for 60 Fifth Avenue, Forbes Magazine) at the home front in New Jersey.

The plane is a prime carrier of the message and its messengers.

You don't get into a balloon to go someplace; you get into a balloon to be in a balloon. And getting there isn't *half* the fun, it's *all* the fun. The trip's the whole trip, and where you'll end up nobody can know ahead of time. When you're up there, you're one with the sky, and that is really the whole point of this sport.

Balloons go where the wind goes, which is rarely a destination you have in mind unless, to cite a spectacular episode from my own ballooning history, you're trying to go from the United States to Europe in the arms of the jet stream. My unsuccessful transatlantic "Windborne" attempt covered exactly twenty feet, all of it on the asphalt. For an overall cost of $1.35 million, that works out to $6,000 an inch. Instead of going up to thirty thousand feet, we dropped three feet from the launching platform.

I became interested in ballooning one day in 1972 when I spotted an advertisement in our hometown newspaper mentioning that it was possible, for a modest fee, to make a balloon ascension in nearby Princeton. Since the specified hours were early in the morning, and since I leave for New York before six, I said to my driver, "Let's do it."

We arrived in Princeton on the agreed-upon morning, and the two of us watched as the colorful balloon was spread out on the ground and inflated. We climbed into the basket, floated over Princeton as the sun was coming up and landed on somebody's lawn forty-five minutes later.

I was completely hooked.

It reminded me of going to the circus as a kid and being given one of those little helium-filled balloons. It would be tied to your wrist and someone would say, "Hang on to it, or you'll lose it." You were torn because a part of you didn't want to lose it, but you *wanted* to let it go and watch it soar away. And you fantasized about soaring away with it.

Well, when you're a balloonist, you're at the other end of the string. You *do* go with it. Like Peter Pan, you *do* float away a little above treetop level. People say hello, dogs bark, deer bound. You ask where you are and someone

"Minutes before I found I could walk on water."
(See page 133)

explains you're in a balloon and everybody smiles and waves as you float by in this lovely Christmas ornament come alive.

That morning the two of us were so high on balloons after our maiden flight that we both signed up for instruction, and three months later we had our licenses. In those days, balloon-flying requirements were basically the same as for a small-plane pilot's license—weather observation, map-reading, how to compute distances, that sort of thing—but the sport was so embryonic that for the balloon questions nobody could agree on the correct answers. Everybody seemed to have an opinion, but there simply wasn't enough pooled experience for the Federal Aviation Administration to have any real expertise. All that has changed now.

Right from the beginning, ballooning became an addiction for me. I commissioned a balloon bearing the slogan CAPITALIST TOOL, and it arrived two days after my license. We've been ardent balloonatics ever since.

My interest in the huge fantasy-shaped balloons that have become a speciality of the Forbes Friendship Visits to foreign lands began with our first Friendship Tour to China, in 1982. Only Armand Hammer was able to arrange our visit, after former President Nixon as well as Henry Kissinger had struck out trying on our behalf. We sallied forth in a balloon decorated with crossed U.S. and Chinese flags bearing the legend "Forbes salutes U.S.-China friendship" in huge Chinese characters.

It was conventionally shaped, but the next year we toured Pakistan at the invitation of its leader, the late President Zia, on a balloon/motorcycle visit, and for that occasion Britain's master balloon-maker Don Cameron constructed the tallest balloon ever built: a 210-foot replica of the Minar, Pakistan's freedom monument. It looks like a blend of the Eiffel Tower and a minaret and turned out to be extremely impressive, difficult to inflate and even harder to fly. Our replica ended up being ten feet taller than the original. It made a great hit with the Pakistanis once we learned how to get it up.

After Pakistan, our next trip was to Egypt, and for that tour Don built a replica of the Sphinx, which we inflated in the shade of the real Sphinx and flew over Cairo and other major cities as well as over areas of the Sinai Desert.

Thailand was our destination the following year, a trip that gave birth to *The Great Sky Elephant*, a balloon version of the country's national and royal symbol. Other Friendship trips have spawned a replica of the *Golden Temple* of Kyoto, which we flew over Mount Fuji and several of Japan's foremost cities; a hot-air bust of *Beethoven*, which captured the imaginations of both the West and East Germans; and, most recently, a towering reincarnation of *Suleyman* the Magnificent, in celebration of our 1988 Friendship Tour to Turkey. This year it's a fabulous flying replica of the *Santa Maria*, saluting Spain in advance of 1992 festivals to mark the

In Thailand, elephants are royal.

The Minar.

Pakistan's late Zia decorates MF.

Lifting a Fabergé Imperial egg.

Columbus returns to Spain by sky.

five-hundredth anniversary of Columbus' discovery of America.

The whole shaped-balloon enterprise grew to be such a gas that we feared we could not limit ourselves to only one a year, and so we didn't. Because of my interest in cycling, a two-hundred-foot-long replica of a Harley-Davidson Softail cycle joined the squadron, and, to commemorate an exhibition of our Fabergé eggs at Baron Thyssen's magnificent castle in Switzerland, an airborne version of an Imperial Easter Egg, the *Rosebud Egg*, was hatched.

But perhaps the best known of all of Don Cameron's flights of imagination is the eye-stunning reproduction of the Forbes-owned seventeenth-century Château de Balleroy in Normandy, France. When we fly it at the real

château, it is a sight that never fails to startle the unwary, for it looks like just what it is—a floating castle. Seeing the two of them together provides a real kick.

Each year at Balleroy—which is just twenty-six miles from the World War II D-Day landing beaches—we debut the year's newest model at our annual International Balloon Meet, to which we invite outstanding balloonists from every country that participates in the sport. At Balle-

Which is which?

The Sphinx over Cairo.

Inside looking out at the laboring crew.

Sometimes he creates new openings.

The balloons give everyone a lift.

In Hamburg, no wind and a ticket for blocking traffic.

From the outside, the laboring crew looks in.

ABOVE AND BEYOND · 131

Inside out.

roy, too, is the world's first all-balloon museum, installed in a nearly four-centuries-old Mansart-designed stable.

It was two French brothers, the Montgolfiers, who conceived the sport of ballooning by observing how a scrap of paper in a fireplace would flutter and dance above the flame. The Mongolfiers resolved to try to understand and harness the principle. They thought at first that it was the smoke that made the paper rise, but eventually determined it was heated air that provided the lift.

Their early balloons, which were constructed out of papier-mâché or linen, used bonfire-heated air and were extremely flammable. As time went on, it was discovered that hydrogen, which is even lighter than air, could be used in place of it, thus eliminating the danger of open flames. Hydrogen's considerable cost limited the sport, however, and it was left to balloonist pioneers in America after World War II to perfect the handy propane systems that we use today.

The main differences between gas balloons and the hot-air variety that we fly are cost and convenience. With gas balloons, sand is dumped in order for the balloon to rise, and hydrogen or helium is vented to descend; with hot-air balloons, height is controlled by heating the air or letting it cool. Gas is more cumbersome, but the ride is wonderfully serene and noiseless. It costs a lot more than hot air. You can fly for hours on about $100 worth of propane, but with gas when you go home for supper $1,000 worth of hydrogen is gone with the wind.

After happily pursuing the sport for fifteen years, I still find ballooning to be far and away the most gloriously frivolous endeavor one can enjoy. Ballooning serves no useful purpose except to make people smile and dogs bark. It takes place outdoors, is enormously colorful and is a joyride in the truest sense of the word.

Ballooning can also lead to deep personal enlightenment, as it did for me at the conclusion of my west-to-east hot-air-balloon trip across the country in 1973: thirty-four days, 2,911 nautical miles—and a page in the history book of ballooning.

I had anticipated that crossing the Rockies would be tough, but it really wasn't so bad. There were other challenges that were worse. At times I would wonder why I was doing it. "Why am I here?" I'd ask myself, but then the sun would rise and so would my spirits. My clearest memory of this transcontinental adventure is of the finale, landing on the waters of Chesapeake Bay. I remember thinking at the moment of hitting the water, "Forbes, this is one hell of a way to go." I was floundering in the frigid water, weighted down by layers of winter clothing and heavy boots, when I discovered that the water was shallow enough to stand up in.

Such epiphanies are not to be treated lightly.

If the sea hadn't been shallow, it would have been their last descent.

In Paris, Fabergé's egg lifts 92-year-old Commandant Paul Louis Weiller.

Rising Sun Meets Rising Temple and Riding Capitalists

BY CLIFFORD D. MAY

WELL, THERE THEY WERE, all right, just like the man said.

Lined up all in a row, asparkle in the brilliance of an early Tokyo morning, 60-odd full-dress, chrome-bedecked, baroque, baadaass Harley-Davidsons. And right beside them, caressing, polishing and mainly just showing off these wide-wheeled beauties, 60-plus members of the All-Japan Harley-Davidson Owners Association, also known as the Kings of the Highway Club, also known as the Harley Brightly Society.

The Japanese Harley riders were done up in California Highway Patrolmen uniforms, complete with white pants tucked into knee-high boots, starched blue shirts, thin ties and gloves folded neatly under epaulettes. They had police-style helmets, too, with real police badges on them.

For Japanese bikers, Harleys are the ultimate motorcycles . . .

But a little more about the bikes: Many had sirens and revolving lights. One was fitted out with a hand-tooled Western saddle that would have done Trigger proud. Another had a television set in the sidecar. Several were equipped with cellular telephones and compact disc players.

The cheapest had to cost double the U.S. price. Several would have topped $50,000. "More expensive than a Cadillac limousine," one club member said, proudly slapping the fender of his hog—as massive Harleys are affectionately termed.

These well-to-do desperadoes, along with hundreds of other less eccentric folk, had congregated in a Tokyo suburb in July 1986, to meet and greet Malcolm Forbes and his All-American Motorcycle Gang, the Capitalist Tools, who were beginning the Forbes Friendship Tour of Japan.

The Forbes voyages—by Harley-Davidson and hot-air balloon—have by now become famous far beyond the realms of bikers, balloonists and businessmen. I realized that when I mentioned to a neighbor, a Long Island housewife, that I was off to motorcycle in Japan, and her unhesitating response was: "Oh, just like Malcolm Forbes."

In recent years, Capitalist Tools teams have journeyed through Russia, China, Pakistan, Egypt, Thailand, Malaysia and all of Western Europe—places where, as MF put it, "we had an interest and thought we might not do too much damage."

Part of the reason for the current odyssey, MF was soon to explain to about 75 million Japanese at innumerable receptions and in television, magazine and newspaper interviews, was to demonstrate, during a time of rising economic friction, the underlying warmth and communality that the American and Japanese people feel for one another.

As for the friction, that is largely the consequence of Japan's black belt mastery of the martial arts of capitalism. "Japan probably has the strongest economy in the world today," MF pointed out, "with a per capita GNP that will soon exceed that of the U.S."

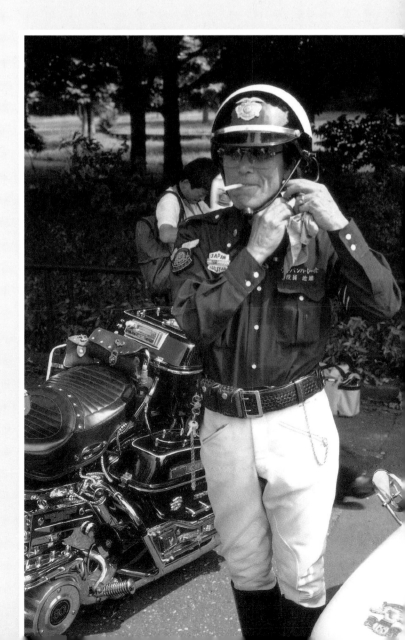

. . . and they load their bikes and themselves with all the trimmings.

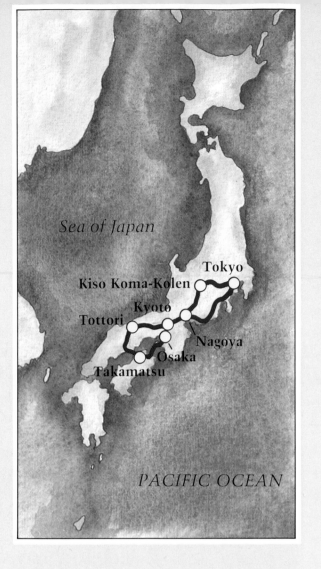

Sea of Japan

Tokyo

Kiso Koma-Kolen

Kyoto

Tottori

Nagoya

Osaka

Takamatsu

PACIFIC OCEAN

Japan's factory wages are already 12% higher than America's at recent rates of exchange, according to a Japanese study. There are now 1,860 Japanese subsidiaries in the U.S. Japanese products crowd American stores, garages and households.

Meanwhile, the sale of American goods and services to Japan has not kept pace, and that has led to pressures in Washington—pressures which were increasing sharply as the electoral season drew near—for tariffs, quotas and other restrictions designed to lessen the huge trade imbalance.

The debate is complicated, its implications far-reaching. But "it can best be resolved in an atmosphere of friendship," said MF, "with all of us recognizing that the relationship between Japan and the U.S. has become a matter of enormous consequence to the entire world."

The other, more obvious reason for this journey was just to have a spectacularly fine time exploring a society that, despite its commercial penetration into our daily lives, remains remarkably murky in the American imagination, a kaleidoscope of geishas and Godzillas, Walkmans and shoguns, cameras, kamikazes, karate, samurai, sushi, tea ceremonies and 240Zs.

Along with those symbols go such apparent anomalies as Japan's renowned postwar passion for baseball and the All-Japan Harley-Davidson Owners Association: familiar forms with exotic content, American images reflected in funhouse mirrors.

A hot-air balloon—the one built for this tour was in the shape of the Golden Temple of Kyoto—would serve as our sky-high greeting card and letter of introduction. The motorcycles, as any rider can tell you, would provide an intimacy with the environment that no other means of transportation can begin to approach.

Getting to Japan was certainly part of the fun. Most of the gang flew over on the *Capitalist Tool*, Forbes' "money-green and gold" Boeing 727.

Once you've flown in the *Tool*, going merely first class on a commercial carrier seems about as luxurious as riding the New York subway on a Monday morning. Travelers recline in oversized leather easy chairs in a plushly carpeted salon. A telephone folds out of the wall by MF's recliner. A video machine with several headphones is available for entertainment. The meals are not quite your standard airline fare: I recall in particular the poached salmon, the filet mignon with wild rice, the Château Margaux 1978 and the chocolate candies oozing Armagnac.

Overall, it was less like flying than like spending the day in the living room of a gracious host. When it was time to leave, however, we found ourselves halfway around the world at Tokyo's Narita Airport, where signs on the luggage carts touched on the tour's theme: "Import now. Imports bring us together."

Heading toward town by bus I caught sight of a fantasy castle right out of Disneyland. "What's that?" I asked Machiko Ishibashi, a Japanese journalist who would serve as our guide and interpreter. "Disneyland," she answered. "Tokyo Disneyland. It's been open about three years now. It's very popular."

The city, as we bored slowly into it, creeping along in dense traffic, seemed huge, modern, crowded, unfathomable, yet somehow orderly, too. Gas station attendants wore uniforms, colored shirts, bow ties and caps. Taxi drivers wore white shirts with ties and white gloves. The taxis had little Japanese lanterns on the roofs, and doors that opened and shut by driver-controlled buttons.

There were gabled temples, mysterious shrines and houses with glazed roofs. But these structures were overwhelmed by the many buildings resembling concrete filing cabinets, all apparently designed by the same school of architecture that has given the world most of its hospitals, high schools and minimum security prisons.

We passed billboards advertising Coke and

Before the Diet.

Rambo—at least some American products have caught on—and watched joggers out for their afternoon run by the massive stone wall surrounding the palace of the emperor: the very same emperor who ruled this island nation when World War II began.

"What a stroke of conciliatory brilliance it was on the part of General Douglas MacArthur to have recognized the emperor's role within Japanese culture and to have left him in place at the end of the war," commented Christopher Forbes (better known as Kip), associate publisher of *Forbes* Magazine.

Kip was often to occupy the passenger seat on the motorcycle driven by his brother Robert L. Forbes, an executive in the corporation's real estate division, who coordinated the Friendship Tour.

Other members of the gung-ho goodwill gang were Curtis Cleland—also (confusingly) nicknamed Kip, Forbes' director of physical fitness; Denny Fleck, director of Forbes Balloon Ascension Division; Jim LaCirignola, *Forbes'* International ad director; Nick Ienatsch, motorcycle racer and features editor of the California-based *Motorcyclist* magazine; Kenichi Katayama—just plain Ken to us—a former Japanese motorcycle racer now working for RCA in Japan; Dave Stein, super bike mechanic in charge of the Forbes cycle fleet, and myself, the Keeper of the Log.

Our first full day in Japan was spent mostly attending receptions, press conferences and meetings. At one point I arrived late at what I thought was a gathering of local reporters. About 70 people sat in a small auditorium across from MF and the gang. It turned out this was only the staff responsible for organizing and conducting the Forbes Friendship Tour.

A multitiered management chart was displayed. Teams rose and bowed as they were introduced. Here was the two-man "weather observation staff" (please hold your applause until the end); the four-man reception team; the seven-man headquarters team; the three-man general affairs team. And so it went.

"Talk about orchestrated," said Bob Forbes. "Sneeze and there will be somebody in place to say gesundheit."

We left the hotel at 5 on a Saturday morning
—MF tends to be an early riser—as a cool gray
dawn was breaking over the capital. We headed
toward the suburban soccer field where the
Golden Temple balloon was scheduled to make
its first flight.

MF had thought long and hard about what
sort of balloon would be most appropriate as a
symbol for this tour. Mount Fuji came to mind
first, but a structure with a broad base and a
sharp peak would make a poor flying machine.
A replica of the Buddha was considered and
rejected. It might give offense to deflate and
tread upon it. At last came the idea of the
Golden Temple, Kinkaku-ji, Japan's most famous house of Buddhist understanding and
practice.

Like MF's other special balloons, this one
had been built by the English master craftsman
Don Cameron. Cost: about $70,000. It had been
sent directly from Britain to Japan with no opportunity for MF to test it. Therein lay seeds of
danger, since Forbes-san no less than our Japanese hosts would have viewed it as a serious
loss of face if the balloon had failed to fly properly.

In the event, however, the balloon could not
have behaved better. At 7:02, with spectators
and television crews on hand, MF and Denny
caused the Temple to levitate into a foggy sky.

The rest of us hopped on the chase bus and
raced through the narrow suburban streets
after it. The immediate neighborhood appeared
comfortable though crowded. Small houses
were pressed together cheek by jowl, some separated by walls or fences. Cars sheltered under
eaves. Gardens grew on rooftops.

Heating up the Temple.

I pegged this as a middle-class area, but Machiko said no, the neighborhood was largely in-
habited by wealthy businessmen and foreign
diplomats. The average price of a house here,
she estimated after consultation with other
staffers, would be between $750,000 and a mil-
lion dollars.

Just before 8 o'clock, the Golden Temple settled easily on the bank of the Tama River, a
placid stretch of water that wends its way
through the outskirts of Tokyo. MF was surrounded by gaggles of admiring children and
batteries of cameras, two of his favorite categories of companion.

Japanese Harley Club.

Mickey Mouse'd girl watches Kyoto's Golden Temple climb over Mount Fuji.

"I thought, 'Why is the Golden Temple in the sky?'" said Masashiko Tanaka, a 12-year-old. "It should be in Kyoto."

"It was just like *E.T.*," 10-year-old Shinobu Tomaki said enthusiastically. "Like when they flew on the bicycle. It must be wonderful to see the ground from the sky."

Many of the kids, I noted, wore T-shirts with inscriptions written in English. Or something closely akin to English. For example, one read: "Come on Sport Stage. Healthy Body and Clear Mind. Be In High Spirit." On a pair of jeans was a patch reading: "Ever blue jeans. All ever blue products can bring you entire satisfaction."

Now, in truth, we had already had some warnings about the mutations that English has been undergoing in Japan. Bob Forbes had sent each member of the gang a copy of the novel *Ransom*, by the talented young American author Jay McInerney.

The main character is a young American studying karate in contemporary Kyoto. Among the conundrums he ponders are shopping bags emblazoned with cryptic English messages such as "Funky babe: Let's call a funky girl 'funky babe.' Girls, open-minded, know how to swing. Love to feel everything rather than think. They must all be nice girls." So this was real, not just a fictional invention.

It was also in *Ransom* that we had been introduced to the All-Japan Harley-Davidson Owners Association, which, McInerney wrote, is "composed of some thousand bikers, most of them pillars of the community throughout the

working week, who on Saturday morning dressed up in Los Angeles Police Department uniforms to ride their Harleys en masse."

Our first meeting with the A.J.H.D.O.A. had come that Saturday afternoon. Yoshiaki Ando, the club's 67-year-old president, explained the existence of the organization by noting that "hobbies have no borders."

The club, he said, has 650 members in 16 chapters throughout the country. Why did he prefer a Harley-Davidson to the many fine and less expensive Japanese motorcycles? "A Harley," he said, "is a wild horse. Japanese bikes are all tame."

The riders eagerly posed for pictures with MF and seriously examined our bikes as well as each other's. "Just like American Harley owners," noted Bob. "They like to case each other's Harley trimmings."

Three o'clock Sunday morning came around awfully fast but all of us were awake by then, heading out of Tokyo once more. Even at this

ludicrous hour there were plenty of cars and trucks on the roads. We passed a skyscraper with a giant replica of a bulldozer on its roof and another building in the shape of a rocket ship. "Space Shuttle Hotel," read the sign.

Misty mountains, the kind seen in Japanese paintings, came into view. The roads narrowed. The smell of coffee wafted temptingly from houses and restaurants. We passed another hotel, this one labeled "Pasadena: That's Where The Night Begins."

Our destination was Mount Fuji, and it was Denny who, around 5:30, first spotted it, a charcoal outline against a burnished metal sky. At 12,386 feet, Fuji is less than half as tall as Mount Everest (29,028 feet), and considerably smaller than either Kilimanjaro (19,340 feet) or the Matterhorn (14,692 feet). But it stands alone rather than within a range of towering peaks and so gives an impression of Alpine majesty.

The road twisted up and around sharply. The landscape was lushly green, Japan's rainy season having just come to an end. A sign advertised "HOW," which turned out to be the acronym for Humanity Opening World. And that, I was later told, is the name of a ski resort. No one had any further explanation.

At the foot of Mount Fuji, statues of animals in police uniforms pointed the way into a parking lot and toward Nipponland, an amusement park.

Denny shouted: "I've got a song here for Mount Fuji, the Mount Fuji song." His motorcycle just happened to be equipped with a computerized synthesizer capable of blaring out any of about 70 programmed melodies. No member of the A.J.H.D.O.A. could match that.

Representatives of Japan's leading balloon club were already on hand, laying out about eight conventionally shaped balloons, most of which would go up attached to tethers.

Once again Kinkaku-ji rose smartly. And as the wind died out, the Temple hung in the sky alongside Fuji as if on a great hook. The mountain peak was now completely cloudless, unusual at this time of year. Whatever gods rule on Mount Fuji evidently know a photo opportunity when they see one.

The clouds had reclaimed the mountain by 8:15 when we rolled out. Our next stop was a rural home for the mentally retarded, where we showed off the bikes to an enthusiastic and appreciative audience. I read the T-shirts. One said: "Big Man's Life Style. Cat Drink Whiskey."

MF made a donation of 1 million yen—about $6,000—to the home. It was actually his second philanthropic gesture of the trip. During the cross-Pacific voyage we had put down for fuel on Wake Island, site of the famous World War II battle, and now a U.S. air base. There is little in the way of diversions on Wake, a tiny atoll with no indigenous population. The base commander mentioned that the troops hoped someday to get a satellite dish so they could receive American television. So far, however, that appropriation had not been included in Reagan's expanded defense budgets. To the commander's astonishment, MF promised to send the base a dish as a present.

We drove southwest among neat fields, small villages and large industrial parks. Traffic on the two-lane highway grew heavy and the air became muggy and hot. Denny played "Zip A-Dee-Doo-Dah" on the synthesizer, which sounded like a carnival carousel.

"Interesting road," said Bob, when we stopped for lunch at a roadside restaurant. "Some of it looks like national forest and some of it looks like Route 22 in Union, N.J." That was particularly true from where we were sitting. Through the window on our right were steep, terraced, green hills fringed by thick copses of trees. To the left rose a forest of smokestacks.

We gazed from one view to the other as we ate our lunches, assorted sushi in lacquered boxes or Japanese hamburgers. MF capped off the meal with a candy bar called President's Lunch. The wrapper boasted that the sweet contained "260mg high desert bee pollens."

The road swung down to the edge of the seashore, where piles of concrete, shaped like the jacks children used to play with, guarded against further encroachment by the ocean. Villages squeezed between the water's edge and the steep, wooded hills that trailed inland.

We passed a hotel built in the shape of a pyramid and another in the shape of a cruise ship. Atop what seemed to be an office building was a replica of the Statue of Liberty. In patriotic salute, Denny played "My Country 'Tis of Thee" on the synthesizer.

By afternoon we were in the Grand Hotel of Hamamatsu, an industrial center sometimes called the Dallas of Japan. A few of us went for a swim in the hotel pool, which, like every other pool we were to wade into in Japan, was no more than three feet deep at any point. There was a sauna a few steps away and in one wall of the sauna, encased behind glass, was a television. So Bob and I sat naked among naked strangers and watched an international ballroom dancing competition. Men in "cat suits," tight pants and shirts with ballooning sleeves, glided across a room with women in flouncy dresses that showed generous expanses of back and thigh. By the time we had worked up a good sweat, the Japanese couple had taken first prize.

"The Japanese are among the best ballroom dancers in the world," noted Bob, himself, by the way, no stranger to the dance floor.

Maybe Japanese prowess in ballroom dancing shouldn't seem surprising, but somehow it does, just as it would be remarkable if Americans were to gain prominence in Kabuki theater. I couldn't help wondering if it wasn't part of a larger pattern: At some point after World War II, the Japanese collective unconscious concluded that if success and prosperity from here on in meant abandoning the Genghis Khan/William the Conqueror/Manifest Destiny approach and acquiring other, newer Western skills instead, then, by golly, they were going to acquire them all, from ballroom dancing to dress designing to golfing to baseball to cost accounting. And a couple of generations down the road, that collective unconscious might have added, we'll take on all comers in any of these events.

We left Hamamatsu on Monday morning heading northwest. (I found directions confusing, considering that China was now to our west and California lay somewhere to the far east.) Along much of the highway we had no view at all: Metal walls rose up along the roadsides, sound baffles protecting the surrounding villages from the highway din. These devices are

Adding to Tokyo's traffic.

now common in Japan, a country where 120 million people—a population half as large as that of the U.S—are packed together in a space smaller than California.

We passed weathered, wooden houses and some with aluminum siding intended to resemble weathered wood. There were boxy, prefabricated apartment blocks with laundry hanging from the balconies, factories, vest-pocket farms, greenhouses covered in plastic sheeting and high-voltage lines strung from stanchions that strode like giants across the countryside.

Bowling alleys were advertised by three-story bowling pins, multitiered golf-driving ranges with nets as tall as cathedral walls and a restaurant designed to look like a Swiss chalet. It was called the Jodel.

The heat was mounting, high 90s at least, and only MF, Bob, Ken and I still wore our leather jackets, sacrificing comfort for a measure of safety.

Gradually, we worked our way through the thickening traffic into Nagoya, the third-largest city in Japan, after Tokyo and Osaka. The main street was six lanes wide, and in every lane the cars crawled arthritically. Where were all these people going, and where would they park when they got there? A Japanese businessman later told me that 50,000 cars park illegally in Nagoya every day.

From the sidewalks and from overpasses, masses of pedestrians watched us and waved. Denny played them a miniconcert. Seekers of relief from the heat disappeared into the Big Dipper Dan Ice Cream Shop, but none emerged with a cone in hand. It would be considered unseemly to walk and eat at the same time.

Vending machines virtually lined the streets, dispensing everything from beer to whiskey to record albums to girlie magazines. Many machines offered the popular Japanese soft drink Sweat, or to use the full name, Pocari Sweat. It wasn't at all bad, tasting something like Gatorade mixed with lemon yogurt.

We passed the Garage Inn, selling "used clothing and junk," and then another boutique named Don't. There was the Playboy Club of Nagoya with an illustration of a cat and the single word "Let's." More intriguing than any of these was the Hotel With, promising "Elegance and Sweet."

By now, we were seriously puzzling over the significance of all this curious twisting and garbling of the English language. The simplest explanation, I suppose, is just that for most Japanese, English words are no more than exotic designs, so the meaning is irrelevant. Would an American buying a Japanese T-shirt care whether it was inscribed with a classic haiku or the motto "3-Hour Dry Cleaning"?

A more conspiratorial theory, however, might take into account that language represents the most important set of symbols a culture possesses. And when one society is vying to dominate another, it often appropriates the other's symbols, drains them of conventional meaning and imbues them with new content.

How many Americans today even know that Kansas, Iowa, Illinois and many other states derive their names from Indian words? How many know what those words once meant? A few decades hence will Americans be studying Japanese English as they now study Japanese business management?

We stopped for lunch at a brown-shingled restaurant overlooking a downtown canal. We sat on straw mats next to low tables as waitresses in soft kimonos served us a local specialty called nabe.

A raw egg is cracked into a bowl and shredded horseradish is floated along the edges. Soy sauce is added. A bowl of chicken broth is set above a flame and brought to a boil. Slices of fish cake, tofu, mushrooms, spinach, cabbage, carrots, green onion and other delicacies are cooked quickly in the broth, then swirled in the egg mixture. Those of us brave enough to try it invariably enjoyed it.

Although Nagoya is a big city, *gaijin*—the Japanese equivalent of gringos—are evidently rare. We had seen few in the streets, and our waitresses were anything but blasé about having us in their establishment. At one point, without warning, one middle-aged waitress pressed her cheek against my beard and rubbed, just to see what the furry little beast felt like, I guess. That sent the other waitresses into torrents of giggles. Though they primly

covered their mouths with their hands, the secret was out: The Japanese are not nearly so shy as they pretend.

We spent the night at a hotel overlooking Nagoya Castle, a 17th-century fortress where, Machiko told us, much of the television miniseries *Shogun* was filmed. With its deep surrounding moat and the golden dolphins on the roof, the castle seemed an inspiring pocket of tradition among the towers and cranes and geometric monotony of the surrounding city.

We were in a soccer field by 7 a.m. Tuesday. MF was giving rides in the Golden Temple and Capitalist Tool balloons to a group of children. Other members of the gang were hoisting kids up on the motorcycles for photographs, horn honking and maybe a ride around the field. All the kids were energetic, enthusiastic and great fun to play with. All of them also happened to be afflicted by serious ailments. They lived at a hospital where they survived only by being routinely hooked up to kidney dialysis machines.

Reception guests sign in.

Several members of the A.J.H.D.O.A. had shown up, in California Highway Patrolmen uniforms as always. One sat on a bench waving a Japanese fan in front of his face.

When we left, about a dozen of the bikers accompanied us. The traffic had congealed into a nearly solid mass of steel. "There's no other highway out of town," Bob shouted over the engine roar. "Imagine: One of the biggest cities in Japan, and there's only one way out." MF said later: "They can't do much about it, the country hasn't enough good flat land. Think of the uproar if they were to use up more land for roads to convenience the rich."

Sitting on the Harley in the sun was like perching atop a furnace. I shed my jacket, comfort finally beating out safety. MF, Bob and Ken more prudently kept their jackets on.

Eventually, we entered Osaka, a commercial hub. A Japanese businessman in Tokyo had warned me that "in Osaka, people run, they don't walk. They greet each other by saying 'Hi! Make any money today?' "

We checked in at the Plaza Hotel, stripped off our sweat-soaked clothes and headed for the pool, which was squeezed onto a ledge on one of the building's upper floors. Among those romping in the shallow water were several American men of colossal size and girth. They turned out to be professional wrestlers on tour.

"How's it going?" Kip Cleland asked one. "Making five grand a week," he replied. I wondered if he realized he was using a traditional Osakan greeting.

The next morning found us in the park by

Osaka Castle, another well-preserved remnant of ancient Japan, where MF was again giving tether rides in the Golden Temple to children, television reporters and dignitaries, more or less in that order.

Beneath trees in which millions of cicadas noisily buzzed, golfers practiced their short game. I read a child's T-shirt: "Bully Club Have a Good Time. Bully Club: This one, this wears. Elect by bully club its the likely dress."

I had another thought about all this Japlish: I was reminded of the poems Gregory Corso and some of the other beat poets used to write, linguistic insurgencies in which the meaning of the words was secondary to how they sounded. Maybe the Japanese were also in pursuit of a pure and abstract euphony.

Arguing against that, in a way, is the number of English words that colloquial Japanese has absorbed with meaning intact. For example, a *nise boi* can take his *galu friendu* to see *beesu balu*. Maybe he'd also buy her some *buanila aisukuriima* or a *chocoleeto milseeki*, which she'd probably spill right down his *way shatsu*, *nekutai* and *burezar*.

We rode on to Sumakou, boarded a ferry and crossed Osaka Bay, landing at the island of Awaji-shima, where a standing Buddha several stories tall guards the shore. The island had the look and feel of a Japanese Caribbean: Palm trees rustled in a balmy breeze, sunbathers frolicked on a narrow beach. Small, pink flowers blossomed along the roadside. The air smelled of fish as we passed the Peter Pan Coffee and Variety Shop. A suspension bridge, under which whirlpools swirled violently, took us over to the larger island of Shikoku.

Although I noticed a restaurant called Cafe Maison Lime Lorry, English was used more sparingly here. We passed through towns where the houses had pagoda roofs sprouting not only television antennas—once the stock symbol for modernity—but also solar panels.

Then came a hotel called the Flamingo Club, whose slogan was "For Sweet Lovers Only." Later, I asked Ken what sort of clientele all these bizarre hotels attract. He explained that few unmarried Japanese men or women live apart from their families. At the same time, premarital sex has gained a substantial measure of popularity and acceptance in modern Japan. The "lovers' hotels," therefore, fulfill a need and do it with enormous discretion. Often, you can park your car underground behind a curtain and proceed to your room unaccompanied. Throughout the hours the guests stay, he said, they need face no one except maybe one old lady who bows a lot as she accepts payment in the form of cash or major credit cards.

Late in the afternoon we reached the city of Takamatsu, sometimes known as the Kingdom of Noodles. There are said to be 400 noodle manufacturers and 3,500 noodle shops in the prefecture. Several members of the gang accompanied the crew to one of these establishments, where we dined on the high-carbohydrate specialty, washed down by gallons of cold beer and hot sake.

After dinner, we stopped in at a pachinko parlor. Pachinko is something of an obsession in Japan. The game is similar to pinball except that it's played on a vertical surface. If you win, you wind up with scores of little metal balls that can be exchanged for prizes—wallets and combs and such—and these in turn can be exchanged for cash at a booth on a back street nearby.

This last transaction is evidently not quite legal, so you never see the clerk inside the booth who takes your merchandise and hands you your yen.

Some Japanese are so proficient at pachinko that they can make a living just sitting in a parlor manipulating the little wheel that controls the force with which the balls are released. I played for a while without really understanding what I was doing. To the astonishment of everyone I soon found myself 3,000 yen—about $20—richer. I commented casually that it was a pretty easy game once you got the hang of it, and silently I vowed never to play again.

Thursday morning, I ordered a traditional Japanese breakfast: one raw egg, a small block of tofu, a few shreds of raw fish, several varieties of seaweed and pickles. And if I hadn't poured my tea into the dish normally reserved for rice none of our Japanese companions would have laughed.

Actually, I liked just about all the food I tried. Certainly, no other cuisine compares with Japan's for sheer beauty of presentation. Japanese food is also, evidently, quite healthy. The people we saw on the streets each day looked much fitter and trimmer than most Americans.

A sophisticated young Japanese woman told me that a year ago she began eating only Japanese food and lost 12 pounds in a few months. Coincidentally, a cartoon in the morning newspaper showed a paunchy Westerner under whom ran the inscription: "*Gaijin* lose weight but always find it again."

One imported culinary custom that the Japanese have fervently embraced is drinking coffee. Much is sold in cans, in liquid form with milk and sugar already added. Manhattan St. brand coffee pledges that those who drink it will "taste the happiness of New York." It also notes cryptically that in Gotham "where the streets speak to you, something good will probably happen."

By 10 o'clock we were on another ferry heading back to Honshu. The ferry's large central cabin was adorned with brass and crystal, plastic flowers and plush purple seats; suitable for both weddings and bar mitzvahs.

We headed out of the port into a crowded countryside. We passed a diner named Warp and a do-it-yourself shop called My Re-Home. We crossed a river on a small suspension bridge

At the Capitalist Tools' reception, Ambassador and Mrs. Mansfield photo-op with a Japanese masked dancer.

painted shocking pink. The NASA hotel, in the shape of a space ship, appeared ahead. We passed a motorcycle graveyard with parts piled up like skulls in the catacombs of Paris. I noticed The Hotel Part 1 Part 2 and a pachinko parlor with a statue of Godzilla out front.

Road repair slowed us for several miles. It occurred to me that in 500 miles we had not seen one pothole.

There was something else we hadn't seen: graffiti. Such defiant and aggressive self-expression, Ken and Machiko explained, was simply un-Japanese.

Beyond the road construction, traffic did not substantially improve. Kip Forbes was counting traffic lights and would tally 66 before this day was done. Denny said he thought it senseless to wear leather when it was so hot and we were moving so slowly. "Might as well wear them when you go for a walk, case you trip and fall," he said in that homey tone that makes all statements sound like kernels of backwoods wisdom.

But MF kept his on. Since I last motorcycled with him he had had a couple of close calls. In Montana's Glacier National Park two summers ago he hit a patch of loose gravel and went down, breaking three ribs, suffering a collapsed lung, a concussion and abrasions. He had also been nicked by the Reaper's scythe when the Sphinx, the balloon constructed for the Egypt trip, blew its top 2,400 feet above New Jersey. Miraculously, the cold-air-filled chambers in the paws, head and tail of the creature slowed the descent to a survivable velocity. MF wasn't about to let such mishaps discourage him, but he did now appear to be exercising a bit more prudence than in the past.

I looked up and saw the headquarters of the "Japan Pen Pals League, director: Mr. Yukio Kisi." Farther along was the Texas Hamburg restaurant and the Sweet Lovers Inn. We sped on through tunnels filled with cool air left over from the night before and then followed the twisting path of a river through countryside that might have been purloined from Wyoming.

The evergreens on the mountainsides were as soft and thick as a fur coat. There was a roadside Buddha with a red kerchief tied around his neck, and a portrait of Mickey Mouse smiled from a storefront.

We were on fine motorcycle terrain and were sorry to see the ride come to an end as we pulled into the town of Tottori.

Outside this city are large sand dunes, a mini-Sahara that stretches 10 miles east to west and 1.2 miles north to south. They're a designated national monument and an attraction for tourists. At 5:45 Friday morning MF and crew prepared for a flight over the dunes.

They never saw them. With 3,000 people looking on, the Temple and the Capitalist Tool balloons got caught in a strong wind that blew them toward a set of power lines.

Kip Cleland, piloting the Tool, tried to come down fast. He hit them anyway. "I just waited for the shock," he said later. Power lines are probably the most dangerous obstacle balloonists encounter. It's not just that they can toast you. They can also flip baskets over, spilling the occupants. They can scare people into doing something foolish, like jumping. In this case, the shock didn't come. The basket tipped, but Kip and the Japanese filmmakers accompanying him held on and prayed. Eventually, the basket worked free and bounced back to earth. Kip and his passengers were merely scratched and shaken.

MF, meanwhile, had managed to maneuver the Golden Temple onto a nearby rice paddy. Kids swarmed around to see but, he observed, they were too well-behaved to leave the paths and trample on the farmer's crop. The balloon crew later did their best to restore the paddy to its former state and MF paid the farmer for whatever damage might have been done.

The road to Kyoto followed an ancient oxcart route through hazy mountains. The populace of the area, largely occupied with farming and timbering, wore straw hats, baggy trousers and loose shirts.

All too soon, we were out of this idyllic setting and back on the Meishin Expressway, again fighting the heat, smog and traffic.

Experienced motorcyclists develop their own styles of riding. Some tend to be fidgety, constantly shifting position. Some seem to be racing, others to lounge. Nick was now riding sidesaddle, both legs hanging on one side of the bike. Kip Cleland and Dave had propped their feet up somewhere around the handle bars. Ken and Denny were riding standing up, stretching their backs. As for MF, he was in what seems to be his favorite posture: He had set the governor on the throttle, folded his arms in front of him and was sitting motionless, Buddha on a bike.

McInerney had written of Kyoto as a "museum city" of temples and gardens. This was the only time I felt misled by him. As we entered the town, we saw the same mix of factories, office buildings, gas stations and stores we had seen in every other city.

But as we explored, we found that the old Kyoto does survive just beneath this hard commercial crust. The city still has more than 100 temples and shrines. Buddhist monks and nuns in flowing black and white robes can be seen hurrying through the streets, rushing, one imagines, toward a rendezvous with enlightenment.

We set out on Saturday morning to visit the real Kinkaku-ji, the ancient structure whose likeness we had been launching into Japanese skies.

Little had MF known when he ordered the balloon that he was stumbling onto a political, economic and religious battlefield. The Kyoto city government had decided that temples should pay taxes on admissions like other institutions. The Kyoto Buddhist Association had decided that a temple is not like other institutions or businesses.

Tools' <u>Temple</u> meets the 16th century.

In protest of the tax, the temple was "closed indefinitely to public visitation," as a sign on the gate read. Taizan Egami, the robed, bespectacled and urbane monk who serves as the Temple's secretary general, told me that the separation of church and state had lasted for centuries—the site of Kinkaku-ji was first dedicated as a Zen temple in the 15th century—and that he was not about to surrender that independence now. He refused to pay any tax.

MF kept a diplomatic silence on this internal affair, but secretly, I suspect, his sympathies were with the tax-busting Buddhists.

In any case, an exception to the temple closing was made for the Capitalist Tools. Mr. Egami greeted us warmly and walked us through the restful gardens of flowers, rounded stones, and mirror-smooth ponds. The temple, we were surprised to see, was almost exactly the same size as our floating reproduction. Scaffolding enclosed it, as Mr. Egami was using the opportunity afforded by the closing to carry out a major restoration.

MF donated $5,000 to the building fund and was awarded a plaque, made from the charred remnant of the original 600-year-old temple, in gratitude.

In Japan there are two major religions, Buddhism and Shinto, and most people, rather than making a choice between them, simply practice both. Shinto is largely concerned with preserving and honoring the memory of ancestors and, in that way, fending off the oblivion of death.

But it is not only ancestors that the shrines commemorate. For example, a Japanese woman who has had an abortion may erect a shrine to the soul of the fetus and, from time to time, even leave toys there. The idea, a novel synthesis of the two viewpoints so dialectically opposed in the West, is to recognize that the fetus has a soul deserving of prayer, even if that soul was not destined to be born.

Shinto shrines can also benefit the living. At a few are statues with uncarved faces. A woman may apply lipstick, powder, and other makeup to these stone visages. Coupled with prayer, this is meant to improve her looks.

Buddhism, by contrast, in particular Zen Buddhism, concerns itself with an entirely separate realm of existence.

In one school of Zen, the disciple ponders seemingly nonsensical riddles, the most famous of which is "What is the sound of one hand clapping?" The second Zen school prescribes long periods of deep meditation. Either way, the aim is the same: to free the mind from conventional modes of thinking, logic and sense.

Of course, you don't need to achieve Zen satori in order to derive benefit from meditation. Even intense concentration—the focusing of all attention on a single word or image and a step toward true meditation—can clear the mind of the customary clutter.

Any devoted motorcyclist understands this intuitively. The real joy of touring comes when the sensations and the stream of images, absorbed without effort, displace all other thought. In this way, there is a zen to motorcycling, just as there can be a zen to archery, making tea and arranging flowers. A similar

MF getting whacked by priest.

idea was explored a dozen years ago by Robert M. Pirsig in his fine book *Zen and the Art of Motorcycle Maintenance.*

I doubt whether Mr. Egami actually expected any of us to achieve satori when he invited us to sit on pillows and meditate. But he did expect us to take it seriously. A small, expressionless monk patrolled the floor, carrying a long stick used for "encouragement."

When the monk spots a disciple whose mind appears to be wandering, he taps him lightly on one shoulder with the stick. The disciple takes that as a signal to incline his head sideways away from the stick. The monk raises the weapon again and applies two great whacks just below the shoulder. He repeats the ritual on the other side. Monk and disciple bow to one another to complete the ritual.

The blows sting more than they hurt and leave no marks. They are meant not to punish but to hone the attention. Nonetheless, we were all a little surprised to see, out of the corner of our eyes, the little monk making a beeline for MF. Four uncomfortably loud cracks followed.

"I'll meditate, I'll meditate," whispered Kip Cleland, willing himself to stone and oneness with the infinite.

Bob, however, bowed slowly, indicating that he wished the encouragement of a flogging. "Hey, look," he explained later, "how many times in your life are you likely to get hit while doing Zen meditation at the Golden Temple? This way, I'll never forget coming here."

A simple, subtle and exquisitely prepared lunch in the monastery's tearoom followed, and then we said good-bye to Kinkaku-ji and Mr. Egami. In the afternoon, MF took the Temple balloon to nearby Lake Biwa, Japan's largest freshwater lake, for its final ride of the journey.

We left Kyoto on Sunday and headed through narrow canyons and along highland rivers toward the mountains in the northeast, locally known as the Japanese Alps. Many other gangs of motorcyclists were out riding, too. We exchanged salutes.

Most of the cars on the road were, as might be expected, Japanese. But foreign cars, the Mercedes-Benz in particular, served as marks of higher status. Among Japanese cars, one of the most prestigious is the Nissan Cedric. That had a wonderful Anglophiliac ring about it.

By late afternoon we were at a Japanese inn set like a jewel in a rugged, mountain landscape. A golf course spread out behind the hotel, and several members of the gang joined the Japanese staffers for nine holes. Small women with bonnets tied under their chins served as sturdy caddies.

The green fee was about $90 a person. MF had had the bad luck to arrive in Japan just as the dollar-to-yen ratio reached its least-favorable point since the end of World War II. Kip Forbes said to me: "You should do a guidebook and call it 'Japan On $50,000 A Day.'"

Japanese prices are awesomely high. Out for a Sunday drive, a Tokyo family can easily rack up $100 in tolls. To buy a house, belong to a club, or to eat in a restaurant, takes a big chunk out of the typical paycheck, which, although large and increasing, is also badly gnawed at by a tax bite that is much larger than that currently in effect in the U.S.

"The average middle-class Japanese still doesn't live as well as the average American, even if he makes as much money," a diplomat told me. "Not from a material point of view, anyway. On the other hand, he does enjoy other benefits. He has low crime, good schools and good health care."

We had arrived in Japan at the start of the dry season, and although it had been muggy, there had never been any real threat of rain. But at 3 o'clock on Monday morning I was awakened by the sound of water dancing on the roof.

I figured it was a local weather system we'd be free of once we came down from the highlands.

About 9 o'clock we donned our rain gear and steered gingerly down steep and now slick mountain roads. Mile by mile, the rain strengthened until it seemed like we were driving through a typhoon.

As a matter of fact, we were driving through a typhoon. For the next 6½ long hours we fought torrents of cold rain and gusty winds. But the heavy, fat-wheeled bikes served us well. No one went down. And by the time we

It was—literally—a typhoon.

reached Tokyo we were exhausted and soaked to the marrow. But we were also exuberant and triumphant at having covered hundreds of miles of Japanese roads without a serious mishap.

There were still more press conferences and receptions to attend on Tuesday. MF, summing up, expressed our "surprise and gratitude at the way this whole operation was accepted. There had been a question in our minds about how the Japanese people would react to something so unconventional as a greeting in the form of a hot-air balloon and eight Harleys," he said. "But it seemed to work. The people we encountered were as enthusiastic and excited as we were."

We left for the airport by bus early on Wednesday morning. The typhoon had blown itself out, and Tokyo sparkled in the sunshine. The city was still as congested and confusing as ever, of course. But Tokyo looked less forbidding than before, more like an attic you would want to rummage through.

We passed the golden arches of a Makudo Narudo—known in America as McDonald's—then Tokyo Disneyland again. We then came to a park where boys in pinstripe uniforms were preparing to play baseball. The teams bowed respectfully to each other. Nearby, an old man was moving in slow motion, practicing t'ai chi ch'uan on the grass. On the seat next to me was an advertisement for a clothing company that called itself Brain Organic Matter.

Somehow, all of this seemed perfectly natural now.

Ich bin ein Ballooner

BY BARNABY CONRAD III

An undercover agent who works in the office of East German leader Erich Honecker recently intercepted a series of top secret memos. We would like to share them with our readers:

Dear Comrade: Reports throughout West Germany indicate a dramatic increase in the sale of neck braces, Harley-Davidsons and recordings of Beethoven's Fifth Symphony. Did we miss something?

Erich Honecker

Dear Comrade Without Equal: Yes, you did miss something. But don't tell anyone. If you think our kids rioted over a rock 'n' roll concert on the other side of the Wall, get this: The capitalists have started a cult around Beethoven bigger than Lenin's (and I do not refer to Lennon the Beatle). A leading proponent of this movement is that American millionaire who rides a Harley-Davidson. For the last two weeks he has been flying a 26-meter-high Beethoven balloon all over Germany. I followed him from city to city. It was incredible how the people smiled and stared upward in awe at this balloon —hence the run on neck braces.

Dear Comrade: Thank you for your interesting report. Since I will be making a state visit to West Germany in September, your next assignment is to find a balloonmaker who can do a 26-meter-high portrait of me. But no smile, please. No Mr. Nice Guy. We're not in the *glasnost* business.

Someone once observed that diplomats and crabs are creatures who move in such a way that it is impossible to tell whether they are coming or going. That could never be said of Malcolm Forbes. Like the Harley he rides, Forbes has four forward gears and no reverse. Even when he travels with something as uncontrollable as a hot-air balloon, our ambassador-at-large, the Capitalist Tool, seems to know exactly what he wants to get across—even if it's just to get his balloon across that dangerous set of high-tension wires to starboard.

Like a blend of Benjamin Franklin, P.T. Barnum and Phileas Fogg, Forbes has redefined the diplomatic mission with his Friendship Tour, a goodwill junket to promote relations in "places where America seems to have problems"—which seem to be many places around the globe.

In June of 1987, Forbes took his show on the road again, arriving in Berlin with two sons, Kip and Bob, and 20 friends and staff members. For two weeks they rode eight gleaming Harley-Davidsons (followed by seven support vehicles) through Berlin, Hamburg, Düsseldorf, Frankfurt, Zons, Bonn, Rothenburg, Stuttgart and finally Munich. In each city Forbes flew an 85-foot-high hot-air balloon (made by the British firm Cameron Balloons) in the shape of the famed Ludwig von Beethoven bust. Why, one has to ask, would a man, even a rich man, want to spend $70,000 on a balloon and then over $300,000 sharing it, Harleys and hospitality with the people of West Germany?

"The Free World's freedom depends in major measure on the close alliance between the U.S. and Germany. This trip, with a balloon portraying a man whose music is known and loved throughout the world, is a salute to that relationship," said Malcolm Forbes as we circled to land at Berlin's Tegel Airport. "Right now German-American relations seem to be going through a difficult period over political and economic issues. This trip is just a good way, a nonpolitical way, to show Germans that we're not just allies but friends."

Two months earlier Forbes had asked his friend Dr. Armand Hammer, who has unique entrée behind the Iron Curtain, to help him get permission to fly the balloon in East Germany. Hammer had previously smoothed the way for the Soviet Union and China trips.

"We wanted to fly Mr. Beethoven from West Berlin to East Berlin, thinking it would be a refreshing change to have someone balloon into East Germany instead of fleeing out," said Forbes. "But the East German ambassador in Washington told me that the balloon might create a 'problem,' that the world might interpret the gesture as a symbol of the potential reunification of Germany. Honecker finally said it was all right for us to ride motorcycles through East Germany but that a balloon flight was out of the question due to the 'heavy air traffic' in East Berlin."

Forbes laughed, then looked out his window as the jet passed over the Wall that encircles West Berlin. His smile faded. "It's pretty hard to get mad at a balloon. It's a happy thing. But there's a lot of symbolism in a balloon. It inspires joy and feelings of freedom, a pretty rare thing in East Berlin, I guess."

At luncheon the following day, U.S. Ambassador Richard Burt welcomed Forbes with a toast: "Nobody else would imagine using a balloon for diplomacy. If someone in the U.S. government came up with the idea, it never would get off the ground. Germany and America have a real friendship, and this venture symbolizes

Over the Wall, East Berliners could see *Beethoven over the Reichstag.*

the spontaneous nature of the American private initiative. This visit will leave an important legacy."

As the ambassador said good-bye to us, the first raindrops began to fall. But Forbes, I was learning, is an optimist when it comes to the weather. An hour later, dressed in a rain suit, Capitalist Tool vest and a Porsche Design helmet, he led our motorcycle gang on a tour of Berlin. Strung out behind him on the Harleys were son Bob; Dennis Fleck, overseer of the Forbes Balloon Team; security man Kurt Schafer; Kip Cleland, the athletics director of Forbes; Dave Stein, who keeps Forbes' 70 motorcycles running smoothly; Cary Crawley, a commercial balloon pilot; Art Friedman, editor of *Motorcyclist* magazine, and his wife, Eiko; and myself. Behind followed the trucks with the balloons, baskets and fuel and the bus carrying sensible people like son Christopher Forbes and Abby and Peter Schoff, *Forbes'* European advertising manager.

As the gleaming Harleys rolled along the elegant Kurfürstendamm, Denny Fleck hit a button on his bike and a loudspeaker sent the song "Berliner Aluf" echoing into the street. Now this is not one of those 8-note horns—this is a horn that plays 50 real songs, a horn that inevitably makes pedestrians smile in recognition.

Entering the Tiergarten Park, the Harleys whizzed by the abandoned Japanese embassy that was built by the Nazis at the height of the war; then by the Potsdamer Platz, where Hitler is said to have committed suicide in his bunker in 1945.

The last communiqué of the Yalta Conference announced that Berlin would be occupied by the Allied Powers. Today West Berlin is still guarded by American, British and French forces, but in 1948 the Soviets withdrew from the Allied organization and have since run East Berlin as a separate entity.

We slowed to observe the Soviet War Memorial, where two Soviet soldiers in greatcoats stood guard, flanked by tanks that had been used in the taking of Berlin. The memorial was built from marble taken from Hitler's bombed-out chancellery. Ahead of us, at the end of the wide June 17th Avenue, we had our first real view of the Wall erected by the Soviets in August 1961 to seal in their sector of the city and its people. The only bright note about it was that someone had spray-painted "Welcome Reagan!" on it, in honor of the President's visit the week before. Behind the Wall rose the Brandenburg Gate, a once-proud symbol of old Berlin.

Everywhere, West Berlin seemed full of the ghosts of war. Even the modern buildings reminded us that one-third of the city had been bombed out. But today this city of 2 million inhabitants is a vital cultural center with new buildings for symphony, opera and modern art.

The Reichstag, a most tragic symbol of Germany's past, was built in 1894 as a symbol of German unity and once hosted meetings of the Imperial Diet, a body elected by universal suffrage. Burned in 1933, supposedly by a Dutch anarchist, the damaged Reichstag was used by Hitler as an excuse to gain enormous powers. It was badly damaged in the last Allied offensive in 1945 but has been restored enough to house an exhibition called "Questions Addressed to German History."

But Malcolm Forbes, who visited the ruins of Berlin in 1949, looks to the future. Parking his Harley in front of the Reichstag steps, he signaled for Denny to start the music machine and in minutes was surrounded by curious young faces. A woman asked Forbes if he spoke Ger-

The Russians are Capitalist gifted.

man. "Schul Deutsch," he replied with a grin. "School German."

He told her about the balloon they would fly if the wind died. But isn't Beethoven outdated, she asked, a figure from the past? "Beethoven will never go out of style," said Forbes, pinning an Order of Beethoven medal on her lapel.

On the far side of the park two cars pulled up and six Soviet soldiers got out, watching us.

"Maybe we can invite them over—it would make a great picture," suggested Alain Guillou, a French photographer who often covers Forbes trips for European magazines. Alain walked over to the Russians, spoke with them for a quarter of an hour and reported that they wouldn't budge.

"Then let's go visit them," said Forbes. We walked over as a group. Measuring friendliness in a Russian soldier is a matter of degrees, usually arctic degrees. The Russians eyed us coldly, but with a glimmer of curiosity, especially when Malcolm Forbes handed one of them a green canvas bag stenciled "Capitalist Toolbag" containing a Beethoven T-shirt and his book *Around the World on Hot Air and Two Wheels.* Alain Guillou spoke rusty Polish, assuring them no photographs would be taken unless they gave the word. The Russian soldiers finally acquiesced, but they wouldn't shake hands.

"Where shall I send the pictures?" asked Alain.

The senior Russian appraised us darkly. Then, like sunlight peeking through storm clouds, his grim mouth curved upward into a smile. "To Checkpoint Charlie." The Russians got in their cars and left.

It seemed a minor diplomatic success. Then Alain let us in on a little secret. "I softened him up by trading a Beethoven pin for one of his military insignia."

Malcolm, always in favor of free trade, smiled.

When it became evident that the weather wasn't going to change enough for a balloon flight, we put our "skid lids" back on our heads, zipped leather and rode the choppers over to Checkpoint Charlie.

The Checkpoint is the most famous portal through the Iron Curtain and a kind of lightning rod for the energies of the East-West conflict. Revving our engines on the white checkpoint line, we attracted a crowd. The soldier signaled Dave Stein to roll back.

"Hey, Dave, he wants you to back up," said Denny.

"Why?"

"You're over the white line, in East Berlin territory. You might get shot."

As the motorcycles roared away, Denny played "Happy Trails to You," the theme song from the old Roy Rogers television show.

At Checkpoint Charlie.

The gang of Tools up against the Wall.

We turned off the Friedrichstrasse into a dead-end street, parking a few yards from the Wall. Every inch of the 12-foot-high cement barrier was covered with graffiti in a half-dozen languages. In German: "Damn this Wall." In Dutch: "I see this Wall and I am speechless." In English: "If you love somebody, set them free." Malcolm pointed to this last message, a line made famous by the rock star Sting, and commented, "That says it all, doesn't it?"

One of the young Germans in our support group, playwright Egbert Deekeling, said to me: "I remember being shocked by the Wall at first, but after a while you accept it, you forget about it. I went to East Berlin a few times, but then you forget about the other half of the city. It's pathetic. With this Wall East Berlin seems more foreign, farther away, than Paris or London."

Forbes climbed up to the observation platform to have a look into East Germany. One of the guards in the armed watchtower was photographing us. Then Malcolm said, "You know, I really wanted to fly from West Berlin to the other side, but if I do it now, they'll put me in jail and ruin our trip through free Germany."

That night the Forbes family gave a reception in the rooftop dining room of the Intercontinental Hotel for 25 key people in Berlin. One was Major General John H. Mitchell, in charge of the U.S. forces in Berlin. When we described our encounter with the Russian soldiers in front of the Reichstag, he said, "I'm amazed they were so friendly, especially after the East German riots connected with the rock concerts on this side of the Wall a few days ago."

Another Berliner, Marie Barbara von Seid-litz, confirmed the unusual situation: "After Reagan's visit, things have been tense, restless. We feel it."

This was precisely why Malcolm Forbes had come to Germany. Over dessert, he gave the first of many speeches he would make on the trip. "Americans have a deep respect for German accomplishment. What we admire today in the German people is the way they reconstructed their war torn country, setting an example of democracy for the rest of the world. We're here to remind Germans that, despite the differences between us that we read and see and hear so much about in America, there's an appreciation of Germany's steadfast support of NATO and the U.S. It seems a timely visit. America and Germany criticize each other over zero option missiles, the runaway American deficit spending and Germany's trade imbalance. But it's a fact that you don't have problems with your enemies, you have them with your friends. . . ."

The speech was warmly received.

The following morning we headed westward through the East German corridor to Hamburg. The East German police didn't quite know what to make of the Capitalist Tools, but as we moved through the checkpoints, we were repeatedly ordered to remove our helmets, show our passports and match motorcycle permits with each bike. Nearby a police dog searched a grain truck while a grim border guard probed the load with a long steel rod.

Finally, we were allowed to enter East German territory. The countryside would have been beautiful except for the tanks, firing ranges and army barracks along either side of the road, a reminder that Berlin is an island surrounded by hostile Red rule. I remembered what a Berliner had told me last night at dinner: "Berlin wouldn't exist without the American military presence. It would be swallowed up like that."

We had been warned to ride single file 100 yards apart and not to stop by the roadside. But when the road widened to a highway, we started taking some chances: We smiled and waved while passing East German cars—tiny machines that looked 30 years out of date—and were gratified to receive enthusiastic responses, particularly from children.

As we came to the last of the checkpoints, soldiers in watchtowers photographed us constantly. Once in free Germany we celebrated by gunning the Harleys up to 90mph—and yet we were frequently overtaken by German speed demons. (Germany has no speed limits on the autobahns.)

We arrived in Hamburg two hours later and checked into the Vier Jahreszeiten Hotel, renowned as one of the best in the world. Hamburg is a formal city, and all the guests were dressed like cabinet ministers or duchesses. Except us. We looked like extras from *The Wild One*. Since we'd beaten the baggage truck, we went into the press luncheon in our leather. A German journalist asked for Forbes' thoughts on the Japanese trying to build up a military aircraft industry. "It would take them at least four years to get where they could produce decent airplanes," he replied. "If they're serious about correcting the trade imbalance, they can order far better U.S. planes at half the price and get them far faster."

Another scribe asked him if he was serious about nominating Mathias Rust—the 19-year-old German who soloed into Red Square in a tiny plane—for a Nobel Peace Prize.

"Gorbachev should not only release Rust but should pin a medal on his chest."

The smile on the journalist's face faded: Forbes was serious.

"Sure! He not only contributed to world peace but to Mr. Gorbachev's peace of mind—it allowed him to fire two key generals opposed to Gorbachev's *glasnost* and decentralization. He's a real hero. He deserves the Nobel Prize for Peace because he's shown both the Russians and Americans that with all our technology we're both really very unprepared for war."

That evening at the Alsterwiesen Park we inflated the Beethoven balloon for the first time in West Germany. Perched in the wicker basket, Forbes gimbaled the propane burner in the maw of the balloon, filling it with hot air. Like a giant awakened from a century of sleep, the great-maned composer rose skyward. Forbes waved farewell, and the crowd cheered.

For almost an hour, Beethoven hovered practically becalmed over Hamburg, watched by an estimated 100,000 people as they came home from work. Boys chased it on bicycles, and a TV crew's helicopter buzzed it. Finally Beethoven landed in a tiny park squeezed between high apartment buildings in the Grindl area. Hundreds gathered to shake the American balloonist's hand, offer him beer and ask for autographs. Children romped in the folds of the collapsing balloon. Like an airborne St. Nick, the Capitalist Tools distributed Beethoven pins and Friendship Tour T-shirts.

Meanwhile, a few blocks away, a Hamburg policeman had to stop traffic when becalmed Pierre LePrieur, who heads Forbes' balloon operations at Balleroy in France, finally had to land the second Forbes balloon in the middle of an intersection.

During dinner that night at the hotel, Herr Wulf von Moltke saluted the flight: "This is the greatest ballooning event since Montgolfier and Zeppelin. In the future, people may call such hot-air balloon campaigns 'Forbes-ing.'"

Forbes responded: "Just so long as it doesn't become a synonym for hot air."

But Forbes still wanted to fly in West Berlin, so on Saturday he and the crew boarded the *Capitalist Tool* plane.

Two months before, permission had been granted by the British authorities to fly on the

Beethoven joins Siegfried in crossing the Rhine.

Maifeld, a playing field next to Olympic Stadium. But when we drove to the gates at the British sector, the West German guards on duty refused us entrance. Forbes telephoned the British command from the gatehouse.

Twenty minutes later an Englishman in civilian dress drove out through the gates, walked to our bus and said curtly: "Mr. Forbes, compliments of General Brooking. Under no circumstances do you have permission to enter the British sector to fly a balloon on the Maifeld."

"Why not?"

"Because there is a big polo match next weekend, and the balloon launch might damage the grass."

Forbes contained his displeasure to reply with a smile: "Please return my compliments to the General and tell him I'm very sorry that he has rescinded his earlier permission to fly on the Maifeld. But we've come a long way."

Annoyed, the Englishman retreated, while Forbes telephoned the U.S. Mission. Ten minutes later an American diplomat, Elizabeth Jones, arrived and said that General Mitchell, the U.S. commandant, was on his way.

We were finishing a picnic lunch when two British military police arrived. "Sir, you had permission to fly, but it has been withdrawn. I suggest you remove your vehicles from the area."

Forbes happily informed them that General Mitchell would be arriving shortly to settle the matter.

Five minutes later the phone in the gatehouse rang. After taking the call, Forbes announced with a smile, "That's the third time I've been told that I don't have permission to fly. You see, it's very difficult to communicate with the British because we share the same language."

The U.S. commandant, dressed informally for a Saturday lunch, arrived soon after in his car with his wife and sons. He shook hands with the Friendship group.

"Sorry to make trouble for you John," said Forbes.

"Oh, I'm just sorry we haven't been much help, Malcolm. But as you know, you're standing on the most complicated piece of real estate in the world."

The gates opened, divulging a dark car. General Patrick Brooking, also in civilian dress, greeted General Mitchell warmly and shook hands with Forbes. He looked at the Capitalist Tools. It was a polite look. "Awfully sorry about the inconvenience. I seem to be the villain in this matter. But I'm afraid we can't do anything about the Maifeld."

A calm, civilized discussion followed about the difficulties of getting permission to enter the Olympic Stadium by another gate. Apparently the stadium manager had disappeared with the keys. It was beginning to sound hopeless.

"What about the original site, in front of the Reichstag?" asked General Brooking.

"Fine with us," said Forbes. Allied solidarity restored.

"You know, in a place like Berlin it's essential we cooperate," said General Brooking with relief. "And John's excellent at that." Brooking gratefully smiled at General Mitchell. Then, trying to be a sport, the British general even allowed himself to be photographed accepting a Capitalist Tool bag from Forbes. "Oh dear, I suppose you'll headline this one, 'Giving the Villain the Sack,' eh?"

Forbes promised the Military Tool a kinder media fate, and they parted with a handshake.

The entablature of the Reichstag bears the inscription *Dem Deutschen Volk* ("For the German people"), and when Beethoven, rising in triumph, was framed against it, he took on a

Chancellor Kohl gets vested.

powerful symbolism. The balloon turned in the wind, facing north, west, south . . . and east. I was moved by the facial expressions of the people gazing up at Beethoven. There was a redemptive feeling in the moment. Even with a tethered flight, East Berliners would see the balloon across the Wall.

Never one to forget a favor, Forbes took General Mitchell and his family up for a short lift, waving to the crowd below. It was a happy flight back to Hamburg on the Capitalist Tool.

The ride to Düsseldorf was a long one, but once at the Park Hotel, Kip Cleland managed to get several of us out running through the beautiful parks of that city.

The next day was busy. The team rose at 6 a.m. for a balloon flight that was canceled because of wind. On a visit to Bonn, Forbes and his sons Kip, Bob and Steve (who had flown in for the day) were warmly received by Chancellor Helmut Kohl, who accepted an Order of Beethoven pin in his lapel. When Forbes handed him a Capitalist Tool vest, Kohl—a very big man—hesitated. "Do you think it will fit?" he asked. He seemed relieved when he was shown the adjustable buttons. Then the reporters were shooed out, and a private session commenced.

Forbes put politics aside that evening to fly the Beethoven balloon at Zons, a small town outside Düsseldorf. Twenty balloons from local clubs joined the Capitalist Tools in a balloonfest that filled the sky with colorful orbs. Beethoven flew proudly across the Rhine River and landed 40 minutes later, flattening several yards of a wheat field. A generous price was established for the damaged crop. Then a neighbor announced that two other balloons had landed on the farmer's field. As Forbes peeled off more deutsche marks, the farmer beamed.

The Capitalist Tool commandoes packed up Beethoven and drove back to a restaurant in Zons where 300 celebrating balloonists and friends were tucking into schweinebraten, strudel and beer. Prizes were awarded, and almost before Forbes knew it, he was holding a West-

A balloonfest preceeded the beerfest.

Pretending he knows what to do with Beethoven's piano.

phalian ham. "I guess that's because I am one," he chuckled. Then the chief of police put a cap on his head, making him an honorary member of the Zons constabulary.

After returning to Bonn the next morning by motorcycle, the team walked to Beethovenhaus, birthplace of the great composer. Still in motorcycle leathers, Forbes sat at his piano and mimed playing the famous opening notes to the Fifth Symphony. "This takes me back to Princeton days," he said. "I always had a tin ear, so I took a music appreciation course in 1940. The Fifth was the first symphony we dissected."

It began to rain as we left the museum. At the Bonn Presseclub, Forbes fielded questions from journalists.

Why Beethoven and not Goethe for a balloon? "We considered him—another great German genius to be sure—but we didn't think his books were as popular as Beethoven's music."

How much did the trip cost? "I don't really know. It's a little like that J. P. Morgan story about the cost of a yacht: If you have to ask the price, you can't afford to own one. Actually, I tell my sons that they're the ones paying for it —out of their inheritance."

Two hours later, near Bonn's university, Forbes and copilot Denny took off, brushed through two trees and again roared across the Rhine in a stormy wind. Landing in a muddy field, Forbes left his crew struggling with the balloon, rushed back to the Bristol Hotel and changed for a black-tie dinner at the American ambassador's residence.

Richard and Gahl Burt had rounded up a star-studded cast from Konrad Henkel (chairman of Henkel KGaA) and Heinz Ruhnau (chairman of Lufthansa) to Prinz and Prinzessin Alexander zu Sayn-Wittgenstein-Sayn, artist Andre Heller and Count Otto Lambsdorff, for-

With Ambassador and Mrs. Burt, and their newborn Burt.

mer Minister of Economics. The acknowledged star of the evening, however, was the Burts' two-month-old son, Christopher Reeve, who smilingly greeted the guests.

The dinner guests at the Frankfurter Hof included a number of cousins of Kip Forbes' serene wife, Astrid von Heyl zu Herrnsheim. To his guests, including Prinz and Prinzessin Bilba Sayn-Wittgenstein, Forbes expressed gratitude for the warm welcome Germany was giving his team. "Our relationship is such a fundamental one that we cannot afford to go our separate ways. Germany is the front line of defense for Europe and for the Western World. We are linked not out of choice but out of necessity. It makes friendship all the more essential. This trip also happens to be great fun."

Günther von Bismarck, a great-nephew of the

Iron Chancellor, stood and raised his glass in a toast: "Your words express what might be called a national need. What your trip provides is an incentive beyond commercial concerns, one that will surely expand the relationship between our two countries: Cheers. Prosit!"

While riding to Heidelberg the next day, the Capitalist Tools were drenched by a thunderstorm but happily toured the magnificent ruin that once was the House of Wittelsbach. Although the furnishings were lovely, many in our group were more impressed by a bacchic curiosity: a 49,000-gallon wine barrel in the cellar. Built in the 18th century, the barrel was used to store all the wine collected as taxes from the local farmers.

It was dusk when we reached picturesque 16th-century Rothenburg. At the quaint Eisenhut Hotel, we ate a traditional repast of veal knuckles and passed an enormous tankard of wine around the table as a one-armed wine steward in medieval dress recited poetry.

We went to bed early, but not early enough: The "Boss" had us up at 6 a.m. for a balloon flight that was, ugh, canceled due to wind.

In Stuttgart that evening the Capitalist Tools joined a rally of some 10,000 motorcycles. Some of these uneasy riders had already consumed their share of beer. They were boggle-eyed as the Americans inflated the huge Harley-Davidson balloon, measuring almost 200 feet long and over six stories high.

Soon every German cycle enthusiast with a Harley roared alongside to become part of the scene. In fact, one group, the Road Eagles, were U.S. servicemen. Forbes shook hands, drank beer and signed autographs with all comers. The next morning we returned to fly the Beethoven balloon with equal success, though some hangover cases looked dazed when they

Balloon boggles beery bikers.

saw that huge face bobbing over them in the wind.

Some of the veteran Capitalist Tools felt right at home when we arrived in Munich and checked into the Vier Jahreszeiten. It was from this same hotel eight years ago that Forbes, son Bob and daughter Moira embarked on the first —and last—motorcycle trip by foreigners across the Soviet Union. That evening the Forbes family dined with the Burda family, who own *Bunte*, one of Germany's biggest news and pictorial magazines, which was printing a multipage feature on the Friendship Tour.

The next day Forbes and his sons met with BMW Chairman Eberhard von Kuenheim and board member Gunter Kramer, who is president of BMW of North America. The men talked of trade deficits and of the German fear of being lumped into the same category as the Japanese.

"Forty percent of the Japanese exports go to America, compared with only 10% of Germany's exports," Chairman von Kuenheim said. Last year BMW sold 97,000 cars in the U.S., 20% of the company's output. What von Kuenheim feared was that economic pressures would affect U.S. political attitudes. Forbes calmed him with the assurance that the U.S. didn't want a tariff war. "Severe protectionism will not happen in the United States," he told the chairman. After a tour of the factory and the BMW Museum (which has a spiral ramp like New York's Guggenheim Museum), the Capitalist Tools rushed back to the hotel for a press luncheon.

After lunch, Herr von Kuenheim escorted the Forbes delegation to the offices of Bavarian Minister-President Franz Josef Strauss. Strauss embarked on a detailed discussion of global politics. "There has been much talk recently of the decoupling of America from Europe," said Strauss, who, as defense minister 27 years ago, brought the first U.S. missiles to Germany. "No one likes nuclear missiles, but the way to peace is not in missile counting," he continued. "We will always have them."

"The solution is to help the Soviets change their system. When two civilizations are so different, there is bound to be tension. Democracy is a system that is natural to mankind. Totalitarianism is not. Gorbachev knows the setbacks in the Soviet system and is trying to change it. We must help Gorbachev with our skills in science and management and with capital . . . But we must make him keep his promises to gain real advances in civil rights for the Soviet people. The Soviets must stop exporting revolution. They must act like a normal nation. . . . "

Balloons and motorcycles aside, finding ways to peace was an important aspect of friendship. Forbes invited the 71-year-old statesman to go for a last balloon flight, but Strauss declined with a chuckle. On parting, MF gave Strauss a Beethoven pin and the Minister-President handed Forbes a record of Bavarian music and a beer stein.

"I'll fill it with a great international weapon —German beer," joked Forbes.

"Bavarian beer, please," said Strauss.

That afternoon we launched the <u>Beethoven</u> balloon from a grassy field near the Olympic Stadium, flying over Munich, then over the fabulous spread of Nymphenburg Palace. <u>Beethoven</u> turned slowly in the wind, surveying the terrain, until Forbes brought him down in a field near a railyard. The people came out to greet him. Was this balloon-flying just more American show biz? The German press had raised that question more than once, but the smiling faces of the people helping the crew pack up the <u>Beethoven</u> balloon seemed to express something else—happy enthusiasm and good feelings.

That night Malcolm gave a last dinner in Germany and stood to offer a toast: "We came to Germany to extend a friendly hand and a warm greeting . . . and in return we received both in abundance. Thank you for sharing the *gemütlich* spirit of your country. *Auf Wiedersehen.*"

Rolling and Lifting a Salute to the Free World's Vital Anchor

BY BERL BRECHNER

Something, I don't know what, reminded me it was Sunday. Sunday mornings weren't usually like this. It was 5 a.m., pitch black except for a crescent moon rising in the east. The eight Harley-Davidsons chugged around the hairpin turns as we climbed the road winding up the hills that surround Izmir, a key city on the Turkish coast of the Aegean Sea.

Diesel exhaust fumes from night traffic still hung heavily in the tepid air. One of the bikes' radios blared Turkish tunes. And here we were, on a Sunday morning in August 1988, off to go ballooning with Malcolm Forbes on the sixth day of his Friendship Tour of Turkey.

And this balloon, the incredible balloon. Even Forbes called it the "most dramatic and impressive" of the nine special-shaped balloons he had commissioned over the years.

Soon, 46 miles and about an hour later, the great sultan rose with the sun. Garbed in blue and red robes and with his 65-foot scabbard at his side, a 15-story-tall Suleyman the Magnificent, the revered 16th-century ruler of the Ottoman Empire that included the land that is Turkey today, looked again over his domain. In the willow and reed basket hanging under 120,000 cubic feet of hot air, Forbes, Dennis Fleck—Forbes' chief aeronaut—and I floated near Ephesus, the remains of a Greek and Roman civilization that is today one of the world's largest archeological sites.

On this morning the air was breathless. The Sulcyman balloon and a standard balloon emblazoned "Capitalist Tool" in gold and green, commanded by Kip Cleland, of Forbes, Inc., hung almost motionless.

Whenever the wind prevented free-flying during the seven-city tour, Suleyman was inflated and shown off as a grand and lifelike kinetic sculpture, the gusts pulling at Suleyman's robes, bobbing his head, waving his arms and tickling his fingers, and the sun glinting off the 750 painted crescents on his robes.

Six days earlier the Forbes party had arrived at 7:02 a.m. at Ankara's airport. We'd just completed an 11-hour trip from Newark, N.J. in the *Capitalist Tool*, *Forbes* Magazine's golden 727 Boeing. Some of the greeters handed flowers to the arrivees. Once inside, accompanied by a symphony of teaspoons stirring in delicate cups (tea is a morning tradition in Turkey; the pungent coffee comes after lunch and dinner), brief greetings were exchanged. Then it was off to the heart of the first city of this Friendship Tour, Ankara, Turkey's capital and, with around 2¼ million people, its second largest city. The Harley-Davidsons, balloons and all the accessories had been shipped over the previous weekend and prepped by an advance party of Fleck, Cleland and David Stein, who maintains Forbes' motorcycle fleet.

Suleyman showed real personality.

The trip had been in the planning stages for months, but presidential politics back in the U.S. made this gesture of friendship and concern more timely than ever. A Greek-American was a candidate for President. Turkey's history of bitter and bloody differences with Greece was causing concern at the highest levels of the Turkish government: Would election of Michael Dukakis imperil U.S.-Turkey relations or result in reduction of U.S. aid to Turkey?

The edible replica was stiffer.

At every stop, to virtually every official and at each conference or dinner speech, Forbes made the point again and again: For the purpose of the campaign back in the U.S., Dukakis would emphasize his Greekness, ethnic credentials being undeniably appealing in a nation where just about everybody takes pride in their ethnic origins. But when it came to international relations, if Dukakis were to be elected, he would recognize Turkey's strategic and historic importance to the U.S. and its critical role in NATO. "Dukakis will be American first and Greek second."

Forbes' initial opportunity to get his messages across came at a news conference in Ankara on that first day. "We come on this trip with no connection to the American government, or with the CIA. We're selling nothing. We don't plan a Turkish edition of *Forbes*. Nor do we plan to purchase any large piece of the Turkish press.

"We come," he added, "simply to salute a long relationship between our two countries.

"The form our Friendship visit takes is one everybody can enjoy. Balloons are happy things, almost as much fun to see as to be aboard, and when you're on a motorcycle anyone can walk up to you and talk. Balloons and motorcycles are friendly objects and create curiosity. Military aid is one thing. But this gesture is in a form all people can relate to."

Later that day Forbes had another opportunity to convey his intentions. He and the rest of the team motorcycled to Prime Minister Turgut Özal's residence and were greeted at the front door by Özal. The Prime Minister had been slightly wounded by an assassin's bullet six weeks earlier. He ushered Forbes and his son Bob, who was principally responsible for trip planning and organization, inside for a private meeting.

On the first evening, at a briefing by the Turkish trip organizers for the visiting Americans, the unusual subject of sheepdogs came up. Bob had warned of them in an earlier memo: "We may have a rather strange problem," he wrote. One region through which the group would travel "is loaded with sheep farms, and the sheep are often guarded by large and fearless sheepdogs." His memo continued: "I've been told these dogs will attack anything they feel is a threat to their flock. Unlike the U.S.A. tire-chasing dogs, these confront the intruder head-on and attack. . . . So let's try to avoid large concentrations of sheep."

Narine Hodge, a doctor from Istanbul who would accompany the group, provided more horrifying details at the Ankara meeting. "They

Paying respects to modern Turkey's father, Kemal Atatürk.

are big, savage beasts with spiked collars to protect them against wolves. They're usually attracted by turning wheels."

Bob's memo had us worried. The extra tidbit from Hodge about the predatory wolves didn't soothe us. It did offer something to dream about during that night's jet-lagged sleep.

The next day the itinerary called for the first flight of Suleyman in Turkey. But before that the Forbes team visited the mausoleum of Mustafa Kemal Atatürk, the founder of modern Turkey. After a number of battle victories as Turkey sought its independence in the 1920s, Atatürk was elected head of the country and instituted broad legal, social, linguistic and educational reforms. In two decades he'd revolutionized the nation. Under a brilliant sun mitigated by a cooling breeze, Forbes climbed the monumental stairway to the impressively great hall and laid a wreath at the base of the marble sarcophagus of Atatürk, who is considered as much a father to Turkey as is George Washington to the U.S.

At 6:00 that evening, attired for ballooning in customary red shirts and yellow pants, the Forbes crew with their police-escorted motorcade honked and weaved through rush-hour traffic, with popular Turkish tunes blaring from one of the Harleys' saddlebags. We turned into a sports complex and began readying Suleyman.

On the stadium's grassy infield, with thousands of onlookers in the stands, a brass band, folk dancers and scores of local dignitaries in attendance, this incredible piece of workmanship was spread. Cameron Balloons of Bristol, England, under the aegis of balloon genius Don Cameron, used 5,000 square meters of red, white and blue poly-coated nylon—more than one and a quarter acres—for its basic shape. Miles of "load tape" create the structural skeleton. Much of its design is gold tape, stitched into place. Each of Suleyman's eyes is twice the size of a human head. He stands 157 feet tall. He weighs, with basket and burners, almost half a ton.

Forbes and his crew, with the aid of five first-rate Turkish balloonists who'd been selected to help with Forbes' balloons throughout the tour,

Suleyman takes a bow.

started the fans blowing. The limp figure began to take shape, the crowd roaring its approval and waving American flags. Forbes blasted fire into the envelope. Quickly, Suleyman was standing, more like leaning, the stiff breezes making him look as if he were reaching for the spectators. For ten minutes he towered above all else in the area. The Prime Minister waved at Suleyman, who bent over and waved back before Forbes pulled the cord to the rip panel to vent the 250-degree hot air out of the Magnificent One's head. The stately figure settled to earth like the melting witch in the _Wizard of Oz_, as the prime minister and his security men motored out of the stadium.

That evening, under the stars, Forbes welcomed the business and diplomatic community to dinner. Key cabinet ministers and the U.S. ambassador were among the 150 guests. Forbes hosted six such events in Turkey, with provincial governors, city officials, local business leaders, publishers and other area personalities attending. At the grandest of the dinners, about 300 people dined with Forbes and the team in Istanbul, the center of trade and commerce for more than 2,500 years that remains Turkey's largest city.

Shortly after dawn the next day in Ankara, with light winds and bright sun climbing from behind the grandstands, Forbes and Fleck

The __Tool__ had a rough landing.

clambered into the basket, __Suleyman__ standing tall and steady overhead. Cleland commanded the gold-and-green *Forbes* balloon with three press photographers on board. Majestically, they lifted, climbing toward the southeast over wires and trees beyond the oval track.

Drivers jerked to a stop at busy intersections to see the spectacle passing overhead. Mothers lifted children to their shoulders to give them a better view. Other folks leaned from their apartment balconies, waving at the balloons as they and a chartered helicopter carrying the Forbes film crew cast their long shadows across the awakening city.

__Suleyman__ gracefully settled on the outskirts of Ankara, draping himself across a sloping field of wheat stubble, high-rise apartments off in the distance, a flock of sheep being herded on the other side of the ravine.

Children ran to the scene, their saucer-big eyes telling of their delight and wonder at this thing that came from the sky. Someone, in broken English, asked if this balloon was flown all the way from America. A U.S. Air Force employee drawn by the commotion said, "There

couldn't be anything better than this for Turkish-American relations." Forbes posed for pictures and signed autographs.

The flight and Forbes' dinner the night before would be the highlight of the papers and the evening news on Turkish TV.

By 10, after breakfast and a change into motorcycle garb, those of us on the bikes checked the bolts and kicked the tires, as the bus with luggage and other tour participants readied at the hotel entrance.

"It's good to be on the road again," Forbes hollered as the Harleys rumbled to life.

Forbes, beginning when he was 48, has been an indefatigable motorcyclist. He has 70 bikes scattered everywhere there's a Forbes presence. Dave Stein, who keeps them all running, shipped a hundred pounds of tools and parts for the Turkey trip. He didn't need most of them. Other than a minor adjustment here and there, Stein replaced a clutch and exchanged one battery among the eight motorcycles that traveled roughly 1,300 miles across Turkey.

The road southward from Ankara winds over harsh brown hills. Chuck Berry rock 'n' roll blasted from one of the big bikes' cassette players. Dennis fired up the music computer on his bike, playing numerous Turkish airs as we passed through each village. We pushed along at 65 or 70mph on the open road, led by "Trafik Polisi" escorts.

The Turkish countryside is a microcosm of what you might find in the U.S. Early one morning you'd begin by winding among gentle honey-colored hills, like those in southern North Dakota. Not too many miles later, you'd pass through a gap with tall pine trees, reminding you of a ride through the Cascades. A hundred miles later you'd have a broad, barren plain ahead, like west Texas, broken only by the blacktop stretching ahead to the horizon. Next you'd climb a hill and start hitting the cool air, and soon be on a road along cliffs overhanging a sparkling turquoise lake.

During our nine days in Turkey not a drop of rain fell where we were, a first, Forbes reflected afterwards, thinking about the monsoonlike weather that had drenched the Friendship Tours of Thailand and Malaysia, the drizzle and

A moonscape landscape.

gray in Germany a year earlier, and the deluges encountered in Pakistan.

Wind was the constant in Turkey, so strong late in the trip during a portion of the drive northeast from Izmir to Bursa that we had to lean our motorcycles 20 degrees or so to the left to counter the warm blasts pushing in from the northwest.

On the first stop after Ankara, a small town named Ürgüp, the waving treetops signaled winds too strong for any hot air balloons. The next morning, in still air, Forbes, Fleck and Cleland climbed into the helicopter on the high plateau above Ürgüp as the Turkish balloon team prepared to unload the trucks. Looking toward where they might land, Forbes, Fleck and Cleland saw the incredible terrain for which the region is famous.

Volcanic eruptions and unusual erosion patterns have created an area that looks as much like a moonscape as anything on Earth. Surrealistic shapes of mud and stone cones, needles, pillars and pyramids rise in all directions. Where there weren't "fairy chimneys," as the locals call the formations, the surveying balloon pilots in the helicopter saw olive trees.

"Wherever we go we're going to be in trouble," Forbes concluded after the ride. The balloon team would try again at the next stop, Konya.

This was the leg of the sheep farms, and everyone on the bikes scanned for the vicious dogs that roamed with the herds. By most counts we saw three of them. One watched eight big Harleys with 16 luscious tires roll by, and then lunged for the bus. Nobody said the sheepdogs had good judgment.

At Konya, winds scrubbed free flight of the balloons; even within the town's stadium, swirling gusts made inflation difficult and tethered flight a risky business. The balloons turned and twisted, and once, with Forbes and Cleland in the green-and-gold balloon, a gust partially deflated the bag, sending the basket to the turf with a jolting thump.

Konya is both a holy city and an industrial center. It's most known for its Whirling Dervishes. At a monastery in the city, a devout sect still practices the centuries-old ceremony. At a special event for the Forbes team, men in their conical hats and flowing white skirts performed their exquisite dance of prayer. Nine of them spun and rotated around the room, with soothing flute music and the trickle of a fountain in the center of the hall the only sounds other than the shooshing of their thin leather shoes on the marble floor. For almost an hour they twirled, arms extended, right hands up toward God, left hands down toward Earth. We left in awe.

On the fifth day of the trip, at the next stop, all seemed perfect for flying. The resort area at Pamukkale rests atop a 330-foot-high cliff overlooking a broad valley. Hot-spring-fed waterfalls trickle down the cliffs. A heavy calcium content in the water has crystallized over the centuries into dazzling white formations and terraced pools, looking like a white stone Niagara Falls.

In the afternoon calm, from a field in the plain below this "cotton fortress" (the meaning of Pamukkale), Forbes and Fleck in the Suleyman balloon, and Cleland with two photographers and a video man in the other balloon, lifted off. The brilliant sun highlighted the balloons as they passed the spectators watching from the waterfall pools of the resort area. But the calm of the valley belied the intensity of the gusts and thermals on the hilly plateau toward which the balloons were being blown.

Forbes and Fleck, in Suleyman, made a bumpy but otherwise uneventful touchdown in a mass of thigh-high thistles on a sky-high ridge. One of the Turkish public relations people, Filiz Garan, a small, attractive woman, was first to scratch her way up the hill to aid the crew. At poolside later, Forbes recalled her arrival. "A vision appeared through the brown thistles. I thought the Lord had sent us a beautiful angel to help roll up the balloon."

While Forbes was pondering angels in the thistles, however, Cleland was in trouble a mile away. One of the photographers inadvertently shut off a burner control at waist level in the basket. By the time Cleland got the burner going again, the balloon had descended to within 20 feet of a rooftop. As he sought a landing spot, winds drove the balloon toward increasingly precipitous terrain. Cleland picked a ridge to settle on and hit the mark. Hard. But a strong gust pushed the bag toward the gorge, pulling the basket through a fence, crashing it to its side and slinging Cleland's hand-held radio and tools to the dirt before it went over the ledge. Like a pendulum, however, the basket steadied beneath the sinking envelope. A strong updraft pulled the green-and-gold bag and its basket out of the desolate gorge up to the next hill.

Cleland saw an open area and went for it, yanking the line that vents the top of the balloon to get it quickly deflated. Still the wind dragged the basket, Kip working the ropes and photographers huddled low, about 100 yards before the action stopped. Cleland climbed through the cables from the toppled basket, stepped into the dissipating cloud of dust and raised his arms, signaling "we're okay" to the helicopter overhead.

As this was happening, Stein on his Harley navigated through the local town toward the hills where Cleland was headed. A local photographer in a car was in on the chase, too, and the Harley and the car met with a bang at an intersection. Stein's quick reaction and seasoning on motorcycles allowed him to take only a glancing blow. The car kept on going. Stein was unscathed; he righted the slightly scratched and dented bike, and continued in pursuit of the balloon.

And so it went. Izmir, with the side trip for the flight near Ephesus, then Bursa, and finally Istanbul making up the three final stops on the tour.

Given the nature of Forbes' trip, and his often repeated admiration of Turkish military power —its combat role in Korea alongside U.S. troops and its strong role in NATO—Izmir was an especially appropriate city to visit. Two blocks from our hotel a heavily guarded granite building, NATO's Southeast European command headquarters, dominated the palm-lined seafront promenade.

Driving across the bridge over the Bosporus Straits going into the center of Istanbul reminded me most of Turkey's critical strategic

With old friend Prime Minister Özal.

Friendship T-shirts for President Evren's grandchildren.

If Forbes learned a little bit about Turkey, the reverse was more than true. Turkey learned a lot about *Forbes*—which, of course, was a corollary purpose for the trip. He might not sell enough subscriptions to pay the expenses, but the exposure to Turkey's business and industry giants would surely provide *Forbes* Magazine with invaluable insights.

The majestically magnificent Suleyman balloon completely won the hearts of delighted Turks. Between Suleyman and the pack of eight Harleys ridden by a happy crew who tooted and waved their way across the land, it's certain no one would soon forget that Forbes and the Capitalist Tools had been there, effectively saluting and spreading U.S.-Turkish friendship—the anchor on which NATO depends.

role through history. This city, previously named Byzantium and Constantinople, had been capital of an empire that, in Suleyman's day, rivaled that of ancient Rome. And today, the mile-wide straits we were crossing, which stretch northward to the Black Sea, mark the only warm-weather route for the Soviet navy into the Mediterranean Sea and the Atlantic.

Here Forbes met the commercial strength of Turkey—with bankers and industrialists like Sakip Sabanci, whose company operates the largest banking, insurance, textile and tire manufacturing operations in the country. In Istanbul, too, Malcolm and Bob held a private meeting with Turkey's President Kenan Evren.

Turkey's rapid expansion and consequent high rate of inflation and debt often came up in Forbes' discussions. "It was valuable background," Malcolm concluded later. "They are wrestling with a tough problem. . . . They are going to have to undergo some belt-tightening for a period, but the dynamic is there." Forbes also sees a tremendous future in Turkey as a tourist destination. "Here's an enormous tapestry of history; exotic cities; stunning, vividly contrasting scenery; unique thermal baths; warm, enthusiastically friendly people. There's no question that tourism in Turkey is going to undergo tremendous growth."

CHAPTER

5

NO PLACES LIKE HOME

Because we have houses, several, I'm often asked where home is. Home is New Jersey. Home is Timberfield, where our five children grew up and where most of my life has been spent. It is home in the special sense that the others are not and can never be. While I love to be—and rarely am—in our other, very different and thoroughly appealing places, they are not home in the sense we all understand.

recuperating from a WWII leg wound and showed up at a cocktail party given by her best friend. I told her then that she was going to be my wife, but it wasn't until several months later that we were formally engaged.

Months before we married we started to look for a place to live. We knew we had to be in an area where I could commute to New York. We both loved the New Jersey countryside. But Englewood was rapidly becoming suburban—too suburban for these two countryside lovers.

I had friends, as Bertie did, who had settled in the Bernardsville/Far Hills area in the middle of the state, some forty miles southwest of Englewood. We went down to survey the surroundings. Two or three times we liked houses that seemed to be available, only to be disappointed before we could agree on a price or se-

I gave Bertie for Christmas this painting by Oldwick's late, good and great Jo Lovejoy, 1956.

When my future wife and I were growing up in Englewood, her family lived about three miles from where we lived. She was the youngest of five girls, and I was the middle one of five boys. I knew her only as a beautiful little blond girl, seven or eight, when I would be riding my bicycle past her house on my way home from school. When you're twelve and somebody else is seven, that constitutes an age gap of several generations.

I officially met Bertie when I was on crutches

cure a firm commitment.

We lived briefly in Bernardsville, but after trying and failing to enlarge our property there, we decided to look again and we found Timberfield. Part of the house dated from pre–Revolutionary War days, and it fit our needs exactly. We poured our hearts, souls, savings and a good part of Bertie's dowry into the purchase. For forty years it has been home base, square one. Sanctuary in good times and bad. In 1987 it also served as the site for *Forbes*

PREVIOUS SPREAD: *The Christmas tree at Timberfield, a 58 foot Norway spruce, began its life as a sapling about the same time our kids did. In both cases the saplings have grown into big ones.*

The library: Nobody ever guesses who painted the picture over the fireplace.*

Living room corner: Isn't this what most pianos are for?

Dining room: Most of the time it's all family when we sit down.

* Le Polisseur by Toulouse-Lautrec.

Under the stairs, Grandma's dollhouse is still busily played with.

Master bedroom: Jon Bannenberg's high tech comes home from the sea. Over the fireplace, Salvador Dali's MF-look-alike portrait of a motorcyclist.

Living room: On holidays, family filled—at the moment, 21 strong.

On the second floor hall walls, the "paper" is memorabilia.

Magazine's 70th anniversary celebration, and it has been the hub for a cluster of other Forbes houses belonging to our four sons and their families. Only our daughter and her husband, who live outside Philadelphia, have chosen other timber farther afield.

When we bought the present *Forbes* Magazine Building at Fifth Avenue and Twelfth Street in the 1960s, it had been the U.S. headquarters of the Macmillan Publishing Company, owned by the family of Harold Macmillan, late Prime Minister of Britain.

The present building on lower Fifth Avenue replaced two town houses in 1925; designed by the firm of Carrère and Hastings, who were also responsible for the New York Public Library and the Frick Museum and who collaborated on the Empire State Building. These now-Forbes offices won a silver medal from the American

Institute of Architects for new buildings completed that year.

When World War II broke out in 1939 in Europe, the British were forced to liquidate almost all of their holdings in this country under the cash-and-carry provisions of our Neutrality Act. As a result, Macmillan sold out to the Brett family who owned the adjacent brick town house on Twelfth Street, but the firm occupied both buildings until 1965, when Forbes took them over and Macmillan moved uptown. It was the Bretts who cut the door through the common wall between the main building and what is now my office, in the Town House. I do my work in the lovely paneled room that was used by Macmillan as a boardroom and for receptions for its more eminent authors. Margaret Mitchell and Winston Churchill, among others, trod the boards in my office in years past at the launching of their newly published books.

This Town House at No. 11 West 12th Street was built in 1847. It is a mighty handy place to stay when late evening events follow a long day at the office. The luxury of being able to sleep over the store is great. And the house's small

174 • MORE THAN I DREAMED

Solace in the cellar.

Town House library: The Big Figures who sit on the sofa don't compare.

MF's office: be it ever so humble. . . .

Town House living room: Where we soften them up.

In the wine cellar, choices, choices.

dining room, the wine cellar, the living room and the library are called into service to feed corporate wheels as we pump 'em for editorial fodder.

Two or three times a week we will invite a CEO to sit down with me and my sons, our publisher and key editors for cocktails and lunch and some off-the-record give-and-take which is invaluable to us. In that way, we have been wining and dining those who are the meat and potatoes of the magazine in the town house for the last twenty-five years.

We assign a silver stirrup cup to the guest of honor on his first visit, and later engrave on it his name and the date of the visit. Then, any-time he returns, he is supplied with the same cup. We don't try to get our guests "in their cups," but sometimes we feel it's desirable to soften them up a little to encourage them to tell us things they might not otherwise reveal. Often, ideas will come and I will ask, "Can we use that?" or "Do you mind if one of our editors interviews you to pursue that point?" I find that good wine and warm hospitality, genuinely meant, tend to break down barriers to candid communication.

On some of these days the place can be a regular beehive. I may be hosting a luncheon upstairs for a dozen, and one of my sons may have six guests in the wine cellar. In the gallery of the Forbes Building next door, we have a larger kitchen for bigger affairs. There we are able to accommodate as many as two hundred buffet style or seventy-five for a sit-down din-ner. Our talented young chef Christopher Long gets quite a workout.

All in all, the Town House pays dividends in every way imaginable, including a happy im-pact on the bottom line.

London is where our editorial and advertising offices for Europe are headquartered. In the late sixties we set out to find a homestead in or near the city that could serve as a core for this important operation and where we could enter-tain people who are important to us in those areas. We were told about a run down old coun-try Georgian house that had been Victorianized.

It turned out to be a design by Christopher

Old Battersea House: Under the stairs, a carved German limewood dollhouse.

Wren, a house that had been much altered over the years and was presently in very poor shape indeed. Called Old Battersea House, it had been given to the borough of Wandsworth in lieu of taxes, and when I was hoisted up to peer at it over the wall that surrounded it, I instantly fell in love.

It was, as described, a very dilapidated Geor-gian house, built, I found out later in 1699, but there was a general feeling that underneath the latter-day "improvements" slept perhaps the finest example of 17th century domestic archi-tecture in all of London's Battersea area.

Until the mid-19th century, it had been the

The State Bedroom: In the bathroom, Queen Victoria's bloomers.

Guest room: Victorian paper for Victorian paintings.

Victoriana collector Kip in a rare pause.

Old Battersea House: It took five years and umpteen £ to restore it.

De Morgan pottery.

home of a series of wealthy merchants and later, had served as an industrial training school. Twice during this century, it had narrowly escaped demolition.

The location was perfect—twenty minutes from the City, London's financial center—and the borough agreed to lease it to us for a peppercorn if we would promise to restore it properly. So, at a great ceremony complete with bagpipes, we handed over the peppercorn, and the borough handed over the house.

The place turned out to be riddled with dry rot, and restoration costs escalated to more than three times what we had estimated. Even the bricks, it developed, had dry rot. And we were uncovering windows that had been obscured since the time of Queen Anne when ingenious tax collectors imposed "window" taxes. At one point, after a couple of years of this, I became so discouraged I thought about selling it to an Arab who might want a place in London. But, thankfully, we just kept going. And after five years the house was beautifully—no, magnificently—restored to its historical condition, with all the modern convenience options cleverly disguised behind period detailing. It has been transformed into a true gem, all roots and history. It functions fabulously, and people love to see it.

One of the finest additions to the house has been the *Forbes* collection of Victorian paintings which now adorn the walls. Son Christopher had assembled many of them for his senior thesis at Princeton. He had convinced me to finance his thesis collection when he pointed to a Monet waterlily painting in my office. "For the price we can get by selling that third-rate painting, one of two hundred similar Monets," he said, "we would have enough money to pay for the whole Victorian collection. Why pay huge prices for less than first-rank works of a school at the peak of its popularity, when major Victorian paintings are going for less than the sales tax on a third-rate Picasso?"

The collection which was assembled under his guidance in Old Battersea House might have seemed to be a case of carrying coals to Newcastle, but it wasn't. He continues to upgrade the collection—it currently numbers four hundred and seventy-six works by 272 artists—and it is now considered in British art circles to be the world's best collection of Victorian paintings. It is open to the public by appointment, and parts and pieces of it are in constant demand by museums around the world.

The irony of the Château de Balleroy, the Forbes château in Normandy, is that during the war I must have passed only a few hundred yards from its entrance drive when I was in the Army. It was then a major American headquarters, having been saved from destruction because the Germans used it for a hospital. I don't believe I saw it when I came across the D-Day beaches a few months after the Allied landing, and never in my wildest imagination could I have dreamt I would one day buy it, lock, stock and moat, from Myriam Benedic, the last Comtesse de La Cour de Balleroy.

I was bowled over when I first saw it. Built by François Mansart between 1626 and 1636, it has a design of majestic simplicity consisting of three parts: two outstretched wings with mansard roofs lower than the center, which is a three-story pavilion topped with a belvedere. Beyond the house is an equally stirring setting: a park planted with an avenue of two-hundred-year-old beech trees, and the main street of the village, artfully laid out so as to create a prospect. From the very first glimpse, Balleroy was irresistible.

In addition to serving as a fairy-tale spot for entertaining Forbes friends and friends of *Forbes* Magazine, the Château has been the backdrop every summer for fourteen years to the gala International Balloon Meet. And since man's first flight was achieved in France in a balloon by the Montgolfier brothers in 1783, it seemed only natural that the world's first museum devoted to ballooning should also be in France. The stable at Balleroy provided a perfect setting. Ever since the Musée des Ballons opened its doors, in 1975, twenty thousand people a year have flooded into the park at Balleroy to meander through the museum and savor the celebration, a mélange of fireworks set to music, exhibitions of hang-gliding, parachuting

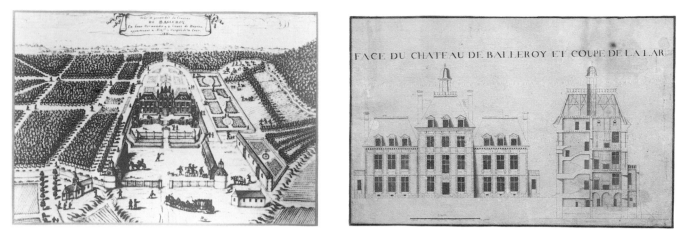

Château de Balleroy: Then . . .

. . . and now. Oldest surviving Mansart creation, built between 1626–1636.

Waterloo Suite: In artifacts, Napoleon wins.

In Balleroy's International Balloon Museum.

Salon d'Honneur, designated a monument historique. Paintings of Louis XIII and family.

Balleroy bibliotheque: Loaded with French rarities.

Palais Mendoub: At OPEC's birth, Forbes *established an Arabic base in Morocco.*

and Norman folk dancing, and, of course, spectacular balloon ascensions.

At the beginning it had come down to a choice: either buy a Brueghel or the Château. Somehow, today I can't envision the Brueghel having provided nearly as much joy and dimension as Balleroy has to Forbes' and *Forbes.*

In 1970, I had it in mind to establish an Arabic edition of *Forbes.* The OPEC countries had become a vital part of the international economy, and the American companies were eager to reach out to these people rapidly accumulating vast chunks of the world's wealth. We needed a base that was friendly to the West, and there weren't many of those in the Arab world. Our first choice was Morocco as being the nearest, friendliest and most dependable possibility. Tangier, which is only an hour away from Madrid by plane and thirty minutes across the Strait of Gibraltar, seemed to be the best place to look.

I heard that York Castle, which had played a key role in the history of the city, was up for sale. I went and looked at it, but didn't feel it

was right for our purposes. Two months later I heard via the Moroccan grapevine that the Palais Mendoub, built by the Governor of Tangier when it was an international city, might soon be available. The Mendoub's heirs could no longer maintain the palace, and it had fallen into considerable disrepair. Shades of Old Battersea, I thought, but probably worth a look.

The physical setting was breathtaking. To your right you could see Gibraltar, straight ahead Algeciras, the southernmost tip of Europe, only twenty minutes away, and to your left the site of the Battle of Trafalgar, and at the same time you could see every ship that enters or leaves the Mediterranean.

Rocks, water and history have always appealed to me, and the Palais Mendoub has them all. It is extraordinary to both the eye and the imagination. Once the sale had been cemented, we made a major investment in modernizing the palace and furnishing and decorating it appropriately under the aegis of the extraordinary architect-designer Robert Gerofi. We also assembled a significant collection of books and maps of Islamic interest.

To the right, you can see Gibraltar; straight ahead Algeciras, Europe's southernmost city; to the left is where the Battle of Trafalgar was fought.

When it was the Governor's palace, three wives had their separate domains.

Outside, profuse with gardens and palm trees.

Inside, a Moroccan street.

Over 100,000 toy soldiers battle and parade.

Bibliotheque: Dozens of Moroccan maps and histories.

When Tangier was international, foreign dignitaries were received here.

Trafalgar Suite: Where Steve and Bina honeymooned, 1971.

Looking out from the breathtaking minza.

In stunning grandeur, here the Governor held audience.

The dining room.

Though the Arabic edition of the magazine has been discontinued, Palais Mendoub's most visible claim to fame is as home barracks for the collection of 100,000 toy soldiers who defend it. They have become Tangier's number one tourist attraction. We don't get to Tangier often, but it is heartening to remember that the Palais Mendoub is silently guarded by what is the largest permanent standing army in North Africa.

It was my bride, Bertie, who introduced me to the West. She had spent summers in Jackson Hole, Wyoming, on a ranch her uncle had bought from Owen Wister, who wrote *The Virginian* there. When I was wooing Bertie one thing became perfectly clear: I would have to share her heart with the West. In fact, our plighted troth included not only a honeymoon in Jackson Hole, but a promise that summer vacations would be spent out West as well.

Shortly after our marriage, we were able to buy five acres near Moose, Wyoming, inside what had become Grand Teton National Park through the foresight of the Rockies-loving Rockefellers. Our acres were close to what had been a ranch in Bertie's family. We promptly built a compact log cabin on it, and our children grew up spending happy summers there. All of us learned to love it as much as Bertie did and does. In the Rockies, either you were a real rancher or you weren't, and for me, five acres, however beautiful, was far from enough to be a real ranch.

Eventually, after much unsuccessful looking, I bought a ranch in Gardiner, Montana, adjacent to the North Gate of Yellowstone. It was some twenty thousand acres, about twelve thousand of them deeded, the rest leased from the government for cattle grazing. It had a family house and a little guest house, plus a house for the foreman and a bunkhouse for the hands. We now had a functioning ranch, and the family began to spend more and more time there and less and less time at our cabin in Moose, Wyoming.

The checkerboard arrangement of the part-owned, part-leased land bothered me, however. The search for a larger spread, one all in one

Moose, Wyoming: Our west began with a log cabin on five acres.

On Trinchera's peak, 1968: A 168,000 acre instant sale.

4-B ranch house, Gardiner, Montana: The first private spread after leaving Yellowstone's north gate.

From the 4-B upcabin, a Yellowstone panorama.

In a Trinchera canyon, a mansion inspired by the Catherine Palace in Pushkin.

piece, got under way.

Eventually, I found it. It was called Trinchera, the largest remaining portion of the Sangre de Cristo Spanish land grant, legitimized by President Hayes, that stretches from Salida, Colorado, all the way to Santa Fe. I flew West in the winter of 1968 for a helicopter tour of Trinchera, and what I saw I loved: 168,000 acres, 262 square miles. Trinchera was all my romantic notions of the West rolled up into one glorious reality. What the imagination could conjure up, the eye could see.

The land was deep in snow that day, but I knew I was irretrievably turned on. Here is a picture standing on top of Trinchera Peak, taken that great day of discovery. My fast-running adrenaline kept me warm.

After we bought Trinchera, we considered operating it as a game preserve. But the sovereign state of Colorado ruled that the wildlife belonged to everyone, and the only way we could populate this vast naturally bounded preserve would be to fence in the land, drive out all existing wildlife and, starting from scratch, build up herds of game.

So, as an alternative, we divided some of Trinchera into smaller pieces of acreage—from two to eighty acres—and sold them to others eager to possess a bit of our Rocky Mountain West. Now a great many have their very own piece of the West. They see as much from their five acres as I can see from our larger patch.

Trinchera's main residence, Cañon House, was acquired in 1981 when we were able to buy 88,000 acres that had been sold off at the turn of the century. At first I couldn't imagine what this mansion's architectural roots could be. Was it a sophisticated version of frontier Main Street buildings that so often faked a second story with a facade? I found out later that the mansion was a pure Texas fantasy, inspired by the Old World summer palace, the Catherine Palace, in Pushkin, outside Leningrad.

Inside Cañon House we have an absorbing collection of shipbuilders' models, along with much contemporary art. The models, unlike the toy boats in New York, were constructed from the blueprints of the vessels whose names they bear. They're true to scale in every dimension

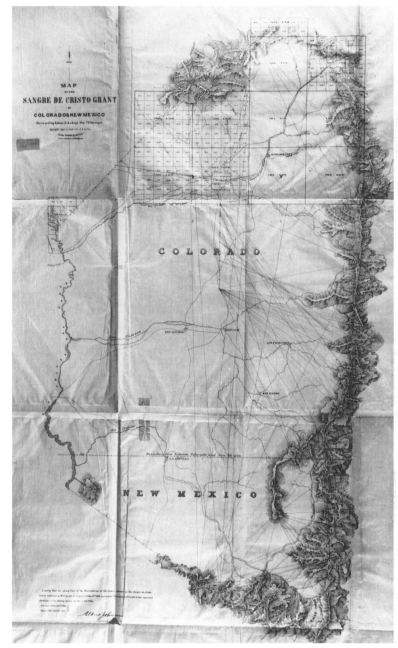

Thanks to a Spanish land grant, 256,000 contiguous acres form a 400 square mile ranch.

—and in every case have long outlasted the ships they were modeled after. Having this major fleet in such an unlikely locale adds quite a different dimension to it.

The view from the Cañon House is a bit limited, but Little Ute Creek has been channeled to run the length of the house and under one wing. All the rooms open to the sound of water.

The main room.

In the entrance hall, swords and bayonets from the battlefield of Waterloo.

Trinchera panorama and headquarters.

Inside Trinchera Lodge: A veritable fleet of shipbuilder models on the Rockies.

On guard at the office, an Indian made in Greenwich Village of chrome auto pieces.

Kip's restored Schley house.

I went looking for a South Sea island as both a retreat and an investment, and the first thing I learned was how few Pacific islands there are that are pleasant, that have potable water and that aren't covered by impenetrable vegetation, guarded by sheer cliffs or composed of nothing but sand.

Why did I want a Pacific island? Doesn't everybody? It's like a teenager yearning for a car.

My fantasy image was Bali-ha'i, but that vision turned out to be more in the mind than in the seas. It was only after many, many disappointments that I finally heard about Laucala. The first recorded sighting of this far-off Fiji island was by Captain Bligh of the *Bounty* after the mutineers had set him adrift. Three and a half miles long, it was the site of the fourth largest copra plantation in Fiji, which was not as terrific as it sounded, because the price of copra, the meat of the coconut from which oil is pressed, had been rock-bottom for some time.

Rumor had it there were probably around three hundred people on the island, living in decrepit shacks of tin and wood. There was no jetty and no airport. The only way to land was to get as close as possible aboard a launch from the nearby island of Taveuni and then wade ashore. Which is precisely how I arrived.

They were right; economically the place was then a loser, but it was a topographical knockout. Covered with a thick carpet of coconut palms and with a range of mini-mountains for a spine, Laucala looked more like Bali-ha'i than the cover of the sheet music.

The island was surrounded by a coral reef which protected it from heavy seas and provided gorgeous natural harbors. There was plenty of water, the fishing was terrific, and even in the then depressed economy the island had a functioning economy of sorts. Again, almost instantly in love with a dreamt-about locale, I flew on to Sydney, Australia, to meet with the trading company that owned Laucala. And that is how it happened that in 1972, the year Fiji won its independence from Britain, we bought our Bali-h'ai for $1 million.

We didn't intend for Laucala to be a hideaway, a place in which to get away from life and living. Instead, we set out to see whether imagination and hard work would make this glorious island self-sufficient. Since the purchase, all of us, Fijians and Forbes', have been working to make the island a going proposition. Today it is a busy, happy place with thirty new houses, a repair workshop, a new copra-drying plant, a general store, a school, a church, a wharf and an airstrip, among other things. We imported a few specialists from outside to help—electricians and contractor types, mostly—but the bulk of the labor has been carried out by the people who will benefit most directly, the Laucalans.

I built my own house on the top of a hill, with a swimming pool. We added near the main beach a tennis court, and, almost as an afterthought, added two *bures*, or guest houses. Today, the number of *bures* has grown to five and we are actively marketing Laucala as the ultimate South Pacific getaway for those into extraordinary deep-sea fishing, scuba diving, or for those who simply want to live the life of Gauguin without the torment.

Our guests have turned out to be a better cash crop than copra, transforming what might have been nothing more than one man's idea of a potential paradise into something like heaven for the people who live there. From coconuts to credit cards, all in one generation.

Plantation House: Laucala headquarters.

From Capitalist Tool Too, *the whole of Laucala.*

Just one of the beach stretches.

Living room.

The hilltop pool.

Everywhere, coconuts.

LEFT: *Our house on the hill: Dining area.*

299   *Laucala bure (Fijian for guest house).*

Methodist missionaries did most of the planting but all faiths use the church.

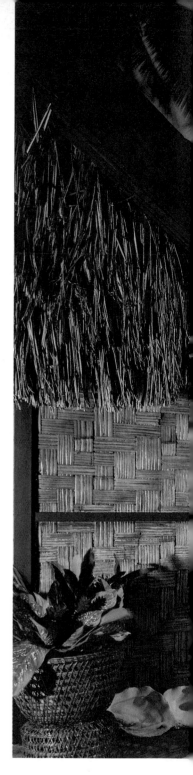

Tin and wooden shacks are long gone.

Giving fear by spear to foes.

It's been said—probably by me—that the sun never sets on Forbes houses, and I suppose that's almost literally true. Do I have a favorite? Sure. The one I happen to be enjoying at the time the question is asked.

Gee, I find myself thinking, this is the greatest. I'm going to come here more often.

Since there are only so many hours in a day and days in a year, it rarely works out that way.

NO PLACES LIKE HOME • 203

Duplicate

9th April 1865

General,

I ask a suspension of hostilities pending the discussion of the terms of surrender of this army in the interview which I requested in my former communication of today.

Lt Gen U S Grant
Commanding U.S. Armies

Very respectfully
Your obt Servt

R E Lee
Genl

April 9th 11-55 a.m.

The within read—acted on—my troops and Genl Sheridan's being south & west of Appomattox covering exits that way—and men at rest—firing stopped—

E O C Ord
Maj Genl

CHAPTER

6

GETTING IT ALL TOGETHER

SOMEONE ONCE DESCRIBED THE Forbeses as "America's First Family of Collectors." And *Antiques* magazine says that I am "a collector of collections."

Well, if they mean in the *numbers* of a family who are into collecting, the Forbeses could probably be *one* of the first. And in terms of setting records for purchases in *many* areas, we might be considered foremost.

Most of the spending records we break are our own. And for a Scotsman it's not a comforting thought to be breaking

At the time, the world's most costly toy.

auction records. But when it's something that has turned us on, we do go after it. There's solace, though, in setting records sometimes. For instance, we had almost three hundred toy boats when the German battleship *Weissenburg* came up, and the keen competition for it led to a spectacular toy-price record—$21,000. There was bound to be substantial rub-off value on the other 299 toy boats in the collection.

Ditto the eleventh Imperial Fabergé Easter Egg, which gave us one more than the ten in the Kremlin collection. Against serious competition, we ended up paying just a bit under $2

million for the cuckoo-clock egg—which didn't lessen the value of some of the more beautiful and more famed eggs that we already had.

Nothing, however, will make me think we weren't nuts to have paid so crazily for the Jefferson wine bottle (see page 212).

Neither my mother nor my father was a collector, and I never set out to be one either. I think a collection—any collection—reflects a personality, and I think the quality of mind that leads to collecting has little to do with acquisitiveness *per se*. Something turns you on, and you never stop. Baseball cards or Fabergé, matchbox covers or Old Masters, collecting is a bug easily caught and rarely cured.

As a family, we never started out to have a collection of anything. Except in the case of my son Kip's Victorian paintings, none of . what developed into *Forbes* collections was the product of we're-going-to-build-a-collection–type thinking. Consider our toy soldiers, of which we have nearly 12,000 on display in New York and approximately 100,000 in Morocco. The impetus to buy was simply seeing at auction a box of them similar to the ones I used to play with as a boy. Naturally, I couldn't resist buying them. Then I learned that another sale was coming up. And another. And another. Eventually, I ran out of shelf room, and out of excuses that I was buying them for my children. We had so many soldiers it was necessary to get things organized somewhat. Because we had an army, it was decided we needed a curator to "marshal" them. Since

206 • MORE THAN I DREAMED

PREVIOUS SPREAD, LEFT: *Lee to Grant: "I ask a suspension of hostilities . . ." April 9, 1865.*

PREVIOUS SPREAD, RIGHT: *Lincoln's top hat and the opera glasses that he was using the night he was assassinated at Ford's Theatre, April 14, 1865.*

At the top, WWII Germans made of saw-
dust and putty. Below left, plastic Russian toy soldiers bought at Gum's
(Moscow's prime shopping galleria) during Forbes' motorcycle Friendship Tour,
U.S.S.R., 1979.

William Britain's American cowboys and
Indians. The background is of mountains
on the 400 square-mile Forbes Trinchera
Ranch in Fort Garland, Colorado.

WWI patriotic posters and splendid toy
versions of that war's soldiers and major
mobile artillery.

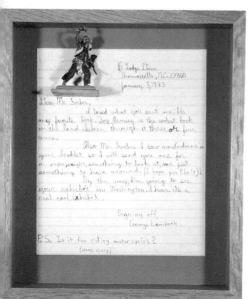

Your head's on the pillow in this replica of Robert Louis Stevenson's "Land of Counterpane" . . .

. . . as shown in this illustration of the Scribner's book in 1905.

then a book has been written, not a book about our collection, but a history of toy armies, of which our huge number provided virtually all examples. For me usually nostalgia is the real culprit, the trigger.

It was the same story with toy boats. I went to an auction where they had toy soldiers, plus a few toy boats. These brought back a flood of memories, so I commandeered a couple. And then a couple more. My children turned out to enjoy them as much—well, almost—as I did.

I really don't believe most collectors consciously start out to be. I think people wind up collecting things—whether they're into bumper stickers or restaurant menus—as souvenirs, as memory-catchers, as substitutes for a diary. Far more fun and far less effort. What begins as a kind of what-not shelf item to recall an occasion or a place is transformed into a quest that rarely ends.

The *Forbes* Magazine Building in New York is where many of our collections are permanently displayed and open to the public. Essentially, the *Forbes* collections embrace eight basic areas: American Presidential materials and related historical documents; miniature rooms; toy boats; lead soldiers; trophies; fine art; and jeweled *objets d'art* from the workrooms of Peter Carl Fabergé. Other *Forbes* collections include shipbuilder models, toy motorcycles, ballooniana, photographs and family memorabilia.

We have a curatorial department of five people who work full time keeping track of everything, recording the backgrounds of the objects, documenting the costs of what we conserve and display and alerting us to new purchase possibilities. Additionally, our curators arrange for shipping, insurance and display of dozens of loans from *Forbes* collections to other museums, other exhibits all over the world. Many of our own New York headquarters exhibits are changed twice a year, and each one has a relevant focus—whether it's the two-hundredth anniversary of the signing of the Constitution or a celebration of Christmas-tree ornaments.

Even more important, each of the collections is alive. None of them is static. We regularly

Ships Ahoy
a century of toy boats

In the galleries' foyer, eight panels from the Grand Saloon of the Normandie *which burned in New York Harbor during WWII conversion to troop ship.*

Three peas in a pod: kids, toy boats, and bathtubs.

Over 500 toy boats by all the major manufacturers berth at 60 Fifth Avenue.

Four days before he died, the Commander in Chief requisitions flags from his Secretary of War: "Tad wants some flags. Can he be accommodated."

When it comes to expense accounts, nothing's new. For his ride, Paul Revere submits his, January 3, 1774.

receive catalogues from all over the world which the curatorial staff assembles and which my sons and I then attentively ponder. With Fabergé, for instance, we add from one to two dozen new acquisitions every year from private sources, dealers and auctions here and abroad. People are familiar with our interests and do not hesitate to tell us when they believe there is a reason for us to have something.

What's more, the items aren't locked away in the archives, waiting for scholars to come and ask for a look-see. They are shown every day so that visitors can share them in an unawesome setting. Nothing is enshrined. The collections are secure, but, we hope, in an unformidable fashion.

Facing such a contrasting selection in our art, some visitors, if they're being polite, will note, "Well, you certainly do have an interesting variety," when what they might want to say is, "What an incredible wilderness!" They'd be right, of course, because in fact I have no devotion to a single period or artist. Quite simply, what we buy has to fill my sons and/or me with some new—or old—emotion, a sense of recollection or nostalgia. When that happens, fortunately, we're often able to acquire it.

Unquestionably my favorite among the collections are the autographed Presidential documents. I think autographed documents—at last count we had some 3,000 of them—are highly undervalued in this country. They make up the only one of our collections that I began gathering as a youngster.

To someone eight or nine years old an autograph meant a signature. On Saturdays during the summer, I used to work in my father's office, and I would regularly go through the heavy mail that he received as a result of his daily newspaper column as well as the magazine. Often there would be correspondence from the heads of major corporations. I was always mightily impressed to see a letter from General Wood of Sears & Roebuck, Henry Ford, or IBM's founding Thomas Watson.

So, I would snip the signatures off the letters and paste them in an autograph album that contained words and signings from schoolmates and teachers. Occasionally visitors of eminence turned up in our home in Englewood—people like Count Felix von Luckner, the daring sea-devil raider of World War I, or neighbor Dwight Morrow, a Morgan partner who became ambassador to Mexico and later U.S. senator from

Original Treaty of Versailles signed by the Big Four (L-R): United Kindgom's Lloyd George, Italy's Orlando, France's Clemenceau and U.S.A.'s Wilson.

Harry Truman writes daughter Margaret's music critic: "Someday I hope to meet you. When that happens you'll need a new nose . . . and perhaps a supporter below!"

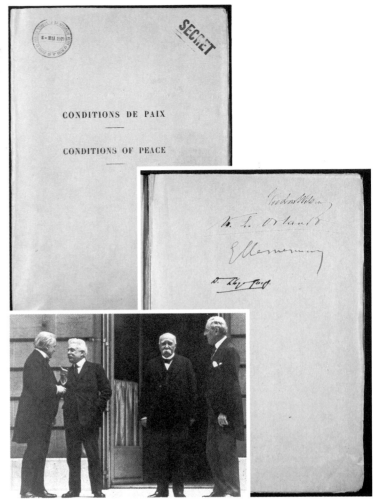

New Jersey. I would eagerly thrust my autograph book in front of them.

So the autographs really had the earliest roots of any of what have since become the *Forbes* collections. And I still feel it's extraordinary to be able to hold a small piece of paper that's part of history in my hands.

The first important autograph I acquired was when I was a freshman at Princeton, and it came through Mary Benjamin, the foremost authority in the field. I went ape over a card she had on which Abraham Lincoln had written shortly before his assassination asking the Secretary of War, Edwin Stanton, for some flags for his son Tad to wave from the White House at the parade that would celebrate the surrender of the South at Appomattox. It was described and quoted in Carl Sandburg's great Lincoln biography. That purchase consumed most of my monthly college allowance for eighteen months.

Imagine the encompassing thrill we have when holding in our hands the Emancipation Proclamation; the Treaty of Versailles; Einstein's letter to Franklin Roosevelt proposing what, in effect, became the atomic bomb; or Harry Truman's outraged letter to a music critic who'd had the temerity to question his daughter Margaret's musical abilities.

Such documents give us in many ways a better conception of a person than it is possible to get from a formal portrait or, in later years, from a photograph. They remind us that these are more than historical figures—they were *people* pouring their hopes, sadnesses, reactions and directions onto paper. Their letters and documents are what makes flesh and blood of key figures in our country's history.

And from such rare paper pieces you learn so much. Take Paul Revere's expense account, for example. We were as amazed as anybody when this came on the market. It covered his

1789
Lafitte
Th: J.

*"The Forbes family would be
far better off if Mr. Jefferson
had drunk the damn thing."*

*Two Jefferson letters: To an Indian chief on the
evils of wine; to a lady friend on its merits.*

January 3, 1774 ride from Boston to New York
and Philadelphia with word of the Boston Tea
Party. By horseback was the quickest way to
get the news around. So Revere submitted his
bill for the expenses of that ride. They were
appreciable, and showed that expense accounts
are not a latter-day corporate phenomenon.
Even at the time of the Revolution, and despite
Revolutionary fervor, somebody doing a job expected to be paid for his horse's hire and his
own lodging—including Paul Revere.

In addition to documents and letters, our collection includes other kinds of mementos and
artifacts. Among the most poignant are the
opera glasses that Lincoln dropped on the floor
of the box at Ford's Theatre when he was shot.
And the top hat that he wore.

Somehow, when you can put your hands on

the things as well as see the words as they were
penned, it brings to stark history a human dimension that makes the dead alive.

Buying a full one of Thomas Jefferson's wine
bottles for the collection caused a stir of a different sort, and it is probably one of our most
unique acquisitions—as to the cost that was
contemplated, the cost that was paid and the
impact it made on the rest of the world. And,
especially, on me. The bottle, a 1787 Lafitte,
came up at auction in London. It somehow
wasn't delivered with the rest of Jefferson's
order. I said to my son Kip, who was going to
be over there at the time of the sale, "Let's buy
that bottle."

Well, he took me literally. The highest price
ever paid for a bottle of wine before that was
around $37,000, and it never occurred to me

that this would get close to that. But Kip called me up when the auction was over—it was evening here—and said, "Well, Pop, I did what you told me."

I began to get a little nervous, because he doesn't always do what I say—none of my sons does, and wisely—but he said, "I got the bottle; I got the Jefferson bottle of wine." I said, "Oh, that's wonderful." When he said, "It was $156,000," I nearly dropped dead—and did drop the phone.

I was on a television program that night for a completely different reason, and all they wanted to talk about was the bottle of wine. I said, "Literally, the Forbes family would be far better off if Mr. Jefferson had drunk the damn thing."

It's exciting to have people feel, see, enjoy these things that we are able to feel, see, enjoy. Sharing them really does multiply the immense thrill of having at hand, in hand, so much that is a key part of the fabric of our country.

As I say, most of what we now term collections were initially modest accumulations. The toy boats and the toy soldiers are prime examples of how happy memories of childhood hours spent playing with both were the stimuli for these two categories.

And just as avocation can lead to acquisition, one collection can nourish the growth of a companion collection as well. The miniature rooms so exquisitely crafted by Eugene J. Kupjack recreate historic domestic and commercial settings on a scale of one inch to one foot. Four of these unbelievably detailed models are on display in the Autograph Gallery: the room in Yorktown, Virginia, where Washington received the surrender sent by British General Cornwallis; Jefferson's bedroom and study at Monticello; Grant's dining room in Galena, Illinois; and John Adams' colonial law office in Braintree, Massachusetts. A fifth complements the Fabergé collection.

And still other assemblies under the Forbes umbrella are just that—excuses to gather together related objects whose total impact exceeds the sum of their individual parts. In that category I would certainly have to list our collection of trophies, each one saluting a go-getter who has up-and-gone.

Jefferson's Monticello bedroom and study on a scale of 1 inch to 1 foot. 18¼" across.

From the auction block and flea market, mementos "immortalizing" momentous moments.

Again, the rationale for bringing them together was a personal one. I have always found it poignant shopping in flea markets—particularly in London, which has more than its share—when among the teapots and such I would come across an inscribed object. I find these memorabilia irresistible, whether it be a trowel used at the dedication of a hospital now long gone or a lovingly inscribed napkin ring—things that were evidential of a moment, an occasion, that meant much to the giver and to the one to whom it was given.

These could represent, sometimes, very private moments; occasionally, monumental moments as when the workers of a plant, for example, presented to the proprietor's son on his 21st birthday a replica of the factory in sterling silver. Or inscribed bowling balls, buffalo horns, or a deer's foot, the evidence of a great hunt. Pieces of an oar from a great race. Or a general's medals which were, in truth, the story of the man's life.

The recipient thinks—and the givers think—that this will forever be part of his family's heritage. Well, nothing is forever, and so the focus of this particular gallery is the mortality of im-

mortality. Everything in it we bought, most times, for relatively little money, but the perspective they bring to that which is both great and small in a human life is considerable.

A Gilbert Stuart of dollar bill George.

One goes away feeling that everything has its niche and its place, and that nothing is permanent, including the troubles of the day or the year. It has all happened before, and with the right perspective you can go on living, trying to enjoy and enhance the life you've been given.

Not all of our collections are either historical or whimsical. Our fine-art collection of over three thousand pieces includes paintings, drawings, watercolors, sculptures, vintage photographs and a few focused subcollections,

including works by French nineteenth-century military artists, British Victorian artists, Orientalists, kinetic artists, twentieth-century American Realists and nineteenth- and twentieth-century photographers.

In our American Painting collection, I am particularly fond of our Gilbert Stuart portrait of George Washington. Stuart painted his first version of Washington in 1796 and it is an image

DREAMERS AT WORK:

Winslow Homer.

Walter Stuempfig.

literally cherished by me and millions of others from the moment we earn our first dollar bill.

In the large collection dubbed "The Chairman's Choice," there appear works by American artists that *this* chairman considers choice. While my family cannot be blamed for what is there, we did—sometimes—talk over these acquisitions beforehand, particularly when big bucks were involved.

When I was young in this business a half-century ago and urged certain spending, my father used to say, "Son, I have enough money for three square meals a day for the rest of my life. The money you want to spend, in large measure, is your own."

So—sometimes—I say the same when my own sons urge certain sizable spending for the assorted *Forbes* collections. While, in a sense,

Edward Hopper.

these collections ultimately involve more of their ultimate dollars than mine, in the end democracy has reigned. The majority has ruled. As owner of a considerable majority of Forbes voting stock, I can outvote their five votes if it comes to a showdown about slowing down.

There is a decidedly personal reason behind every painting I've ever bought. Which is as it should be, because, frankly, I haven't the knowledge or the yen to concentrate on any one period or artist. I have a single Renoir, a lovely modest nude. To me it is a quintessential Renoir. Even if it wasn't so obviously by Renoir, I'd have loved it anyway.

We also own a small Van Gogh, a sort of consolation prize that we bought after losing out on a larger Van Gogh to the high bidder, Mrs. Jacqueline Onassis. It's not a large renowned Van Gogh, but, like the Renoir, it's quintessential, and I love it dearly.

Quintessential Renoir.

Quintessential auction bidder.

Quintessential Van Gogh.

Malcolm Forbes: The Van Gogh was almost his

Because we used to own property in Tahiti, I bought a small Gauguin, a study of the artist's wife and three children whom he left behind in favor of one of his nut-brown maidens. The Gauguin Museum in Tahiti didn't have an oil painting of his, because everything he worked on there had been eagerly bought and taken away over the years. So we had it on loan in Tahiti during the years we owned Zane Gray's old fishing camp there. Again, it was not one of Gauguin's most famous paintings, but, for us, it had an angle that was refreshing.

Once I had a Rembrandt on approval, and I've regretted ever since that I didn't keep it. It's a small one, but that face still haunts me. I kept it for three months, lived with it and didn't miss it much until I turned it back and it was sold. I've since tracked it down, but it would probably cost ten times as much if the owner were willing to sell—which he isn't.

On the other hand, there is a Rubens in my New York office that is extraordinary. It is entirely by his hand—no "filling in" by students. Legend has it that it was painted as a bribe for the Medicis' treasurer. While Rubens was trying to collect from the Medicis for all the work he'd done for them, the keeper of the checkbook said he wanted a painting by the great artist for himself. In three days Rubens painted our Rubens. We lend it frequently to the Met and other collections. I'm not heavily into Old Masters, but I love that one.

Gauguin: His wife and daughters were no match for Tahiti's nut-brown maidens.

How Milton Avery sees the sea.

How Peter Paul Rubens sees Cupid supplicating Jupiter.

The score on Fabergé's Imperial Eggs: Forbes 12, Kremlin 10.

But, when all is said and done, to most of the public our best-known collection is the *Forbes* Fabergé treasury. As in the other cases, we never set out to be collectors of Fabergé. What happened can be traced back to early memories of my being awed as a youngster by the photographs and history of the Russian Revolution, and remembering that some of the work of Fabergé was offered as an example of the waste and extravagance of the Imperial Russian court. This made an impression on me because of the obvious irony involved. When you think about it, most reigning families are remembered not for conquests but for their support of the arts—whether the Sistine Chapel or great operas. It was the art they supported that often gave their reigns much historical significance.

For Fabergé, great hunks and gobs of precious stones were totally irrelevant. The artistry and fantasy that created these pieces gave them their extraordinary beauty. A Fabergé place setting projects a quality that an ordinary knife and fork just doesn't cut.

I caught the Fabergé bug when I was in London twenty-five or thirty years ago. In one of those totally intriguing, old-fashioned-looking jewelry stores on New Bond Street, I saw a cigarette case by Fabergé. It was plain gold, decorated with the crest of the Imperial Russian double eagle. I went in and bought it—I think it was less than $1,000—a presentation piece to

The cigarette case that led to the Forbes *Fabergé Collection.*

be given by the Czar as a "thank-you" for some small service. I gave it to my wife for Christmas, and she was totally thrilled with it. So thrilled that the next Easter I went to A La Vieille Russie, then, as now, the leading Fabergé house in New York, and bought what we call a "jelly bean" egg by Fabergé. It was small, made of white enamel with a red cross. Again, she was thrilled.

That was our first Fabergé egg. Our first *major* egg turned out to be a gift to the Duchess of Marlborough, the American heiress Consuelo Vanderbilt, commemorating her visit to Russia in 1902. The egg had sustained some damage on the bottom, and it was estimated to go for $15,000. Thirty years ago, $15,000 was a lot of money—it still is to me—but I thought it would be wonderful to have such a beautiful thing. At the auction the bidding went a good deal higher than $15,000, until finally I ended up paying $50,000. I didn't sleep at all that night worrying about what auction fever had done to our exchequer.

From out of the Orange Tree leaves, a singing bird.

The Coronation Egg.

That experience, though, is what got us rolling on what's become the *Forbes* Fabergé collection. The under-bidder turned out to be Mr.
Alexander Schaffer, owner of A La Vieille Russie. After that sale, he introduced himself and
said he assumed, because I had bid so high,
that I was a "serious" collector. He took me to
his shop on Fifth Avenue, opened his vault, and
showed me four stunning Imperial Easter Eggs.
I was absolutely bowled over, totally hooked
from that moment forward.

So, something that I really couldn't afford led
me to build a Fabergé collection that is said to
be the greatest in private hands. The Queen of
England has a most major collection of Fabergé; it probably numbers overall more pieces
than ours. But not as many Imperial Eggs. She
has two and the Kremlin has ten. We have
twelve of these ultimate creations.

I have shied away from giving a hypothetical
dollar value to the *Forbes* collections. But I will
say that in many instances the art we've acquired has appreciated more than some of the
securities purchased for our pension and thrift
plans. And, nine times out of ten, my biggest
disappointments have been the things I wasn't
at the time willing to *ante* up enough to get.

In full display.

Embellishments for the ball.

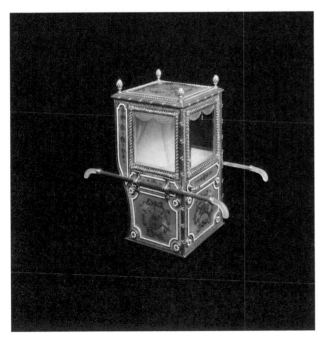

Among Fabergé's incomparable miniatures, a mother-of-pearl handled Sedan Chair.

As long as my kids are alive and care as I do, our collections will not be static things. There will always be new additions to trigger not the desire to possess, but the desire to share something that turned one or all of us on.

I've often told my children I hope that, if they decide to be done with one of the collections, they will put it back on the auction block so that other people can have the same vast fun and excitement that we did in amassing it. If anyone should seek my advice about collecting, I'd quickly point out the old truth: Buy only what you like. Measure a work by the joy and satisfaction it will bring.

If you want to collect as an investment, become a dealer.

CHAPTER

7

R.S.V.P.

Someone once asked me whether I felt guilty about having so much money. I said no, that I felt inordinately grateful and incredibly lucky to have it, especially as I'm bursting with opinions about what could make the world run better and can afford a compelling forum for spreading the good word.

In biweekly editorials I keep telling government factotums what they should be doing and they keep ignoring me with the same regularity

sand-mile learning-and-listening trip aboard the *Highlander* that took us to twenty-one ports in twelve countries—a kind of issue-oriented seaborne equivalent of our overland balloon and motorcycle Friendship Tours.

Actually, there was an important difference between the Friendship Tours and what we had in mind on this lengthy Pacific voyage.

The goodwill trips, with the Harleys and the balloons in the special shapes tailored to the countries being visited, create an awareness of *Forbes* by appealing to the imagination of the general public. Some of that awareness washes over into the business community, of course, because of the receptions and dinners that we

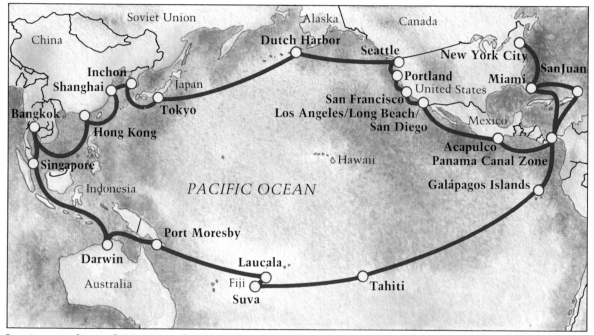

In six months and 30,000 miles, 2,000 rulers and ruled wined and dined.

with which I advise them. It's great to be able to afford our many overseas Friendship Tours, but I certainly don't consider myself a roving free-lance ambassador, because as soon as you start thinking that way you sacrifice your coveted amateur status. Basically, I think I'm just somebody with enthusiasm about recognizing friends of the USA who are so vital to the free world.

All of which may explain in part, at least, how and why we came to launch our *Forbes* 1988 Pacific Rim odyssey, a six-month, thirty-thou-

stage for key leaders and their wives along the way. But the primary emphasis—and the payback—is the familiarity we're creating for the magazine. Naturally, we hope that we may be cultivating future news sources as well, but the Friendship Tours are really mostly about, well, friendship.

So why, in these tight-money times, did we not-so-suddenly decide to orchestrate a serious, time-consuming, logistically complex and very expensive voyage that would take us so far from the shores of corporate America?

226 • MORE THAN I DREAMED

PREVIOUS SPREAD: *Bagpipers, fireworks, kilts and Elizabeth celebrate* Forbes *Magazine's 70th anniversary at Timberfield.*

Jean MacArthur and Kuniko Kusumoto: Panama's General Noriega would have been no match for her General.

Tim Forbes videos the transit.

The Galápagos' turtles were equally curious (L-R): Sam Kusumoto, Sonia Grinberg, Tim Forbes, Jean MacArthur, MF, Kuniko Kusumoto, Gerry Grinberg (kneeling), Uwe Schwarzwälder, and Bob Devine.

Iguana: Ecuador is preserving the species.

Sez who?

For Gauguin they only wore flowers.

Off Tahiti's ruggedly grand shore.

On the road to welcome the Highlander, *Fiji's Prime Minister and Minister for Foreign Affairs, Ratu Sir Kamisese Mara, MF and Islands' former Governor General, now President, Ratu Sir Penaia Ganilau.*

Quite simply, because the countries rimming the Pacific are increasingly where it's at these days for the businesses of America and for every multinational corporation.

Our high-tech age has reduced the vast dimensions of the Pacific to the point where we all are close neighbors when it comes to economic matters, and what happens in or to any one of us affects us all.

You don't have to be a *Forbes* subscriber to realize that the countries that rim the Pacific Ocean are having a dynamite impact on the United States and world economies. And as more of them burgeon, they will be increasingly altering the world's economic-power equations.

The Pacific Rimmers are on a roll whose foreseeable dimensions are unmeasurable, and all of us felt that the quicker we grew aware of the scope of *what's* ahead there, the sooner we could all be a sizable part of *who's* ahead there.

Also, looking ahead a bit, we believe that our already flourishing West Coast could have an ever-brighter future if we could aggressively tune in to the who and how of what's happening on our vast Pacific doorstep.

Then, too, there was the *Highlander*. As serious as our motives were, the kind of mission we wanted to undertake seemed pretty exciting when we had the means and the time and a platform such as the *Highlander* from which to look and listen.

We were also pretty sure that in visiting the places we wanted to go to—Singapore, Thailand, Hong Kong, Shanghai, Inchon and Tokyo,

among others—the *Highlander* would help us attract the people we wanted to be able to talk to: the movers, the shakers, and corporate potentates.

Experience had shown us over and over that in a normal, across-the-desk-type of discussion,

With traditional dances and special verses, mothers and children convey traditional welcome.

With no flies on Laucala, the Tool does the buzzing.

Honking the horn. A Fijian blows his conch.

King of naught he surveys.

From the old days, a fierce spear dance.

Pipes and kilt among native drums and sulus.

L-R: Bill Kasch, Iris Love, Liz Smith, Arthur and Paige Rense, Bob's stepson Miguel with friend Russell, Kip's daughter Charlotte and his wife Astrid, Kurt Schafer, Glenn Ellison.

everybody's a little bit on guard. When a man's in his office, he's more conscious of image and dignity. He's *en garde*, reserved. But on a boat you can thaw him out.

It turned out we were right. The *Highlander* provided us with an exceptionally appealing and exciting means of conveying the keen interest and the goodwill that Americans and America feel toward our Pacific neighbors.

We left on January 21 of 1988, proceeded down the East Coast, did our first bit of entertaining in Puerto Rico (which resulted in a sixteen-page special section of *Forbes* and $331,585 in revenue), went on through the Panama Canal, made brief landfalls at the Galápa-

gos Islands, Tahiti, Fiji, and Port Darwin in Australia and then really started to work our fact-finding itinerary.

Throughout our floating house-party-cum-seminar, we used the *Capitalist Tool* to ferry Forbes' and various U.S. guests to and from the States and major ports of call. On different legs of our odyssey, my sons and I were joined in hosting and taking soundings by many eminences from this country, including General Motors Chairman Roger Smith and Apple Computer Chairman John Sculley and their wives; Minolta's Sam Kusumoto and his wife; Ambassador Roosevelt, the then U.S. Chief of Protocol, and her husband, Archibald; Mrs. Douglas MacArthur; His Majesty King Simeon and

The Highlander *at Laucala: Captain Bligh saw it first.*

MF with Fiji's Minister for Home Affairs, Brigadier General Sitiveni Rabuka.

Dishing it out.

Wake Island's Queen for the day.

In Bangkok, temples and worshippers.

L-R: Archie and Lucky Roosevelt, Kip (foreground), MF, Elizabeth, John Sculley, Barbara and Roger Smith.

Queen Margarita (former monarchs of Bulgaria); Governor Michael Castle of Delaware; and our most charming nonbusiness type on the entire guest list, Elizabeth Taylor (for whom the Prime Minister of Thailand enthusiastically redecorated the state dining room in Elizabeth-inspired purple).

At every stop we explained and reemphasized our original objective: we were there to salute and to strengthen the friendship and understanding that are more and more vital to the economic well-being of us all.

At the end of the voyage last August, we took inventory and found that the *Highlander* had consumed some 210,000 gallons of fuel, and that we and our two thousand guests had dispatched 3,000 pounds of beef, lamb and pork, 100 cases of wine and I've forgotten how many pounds of caviar. All that and a yacht that is not tax deductible.

The Pacific Rim trip was bigger than any of our other ventures, in terms of cost and in terms of potential and lasting significance, both to *Forbes* and to the increase of knowledge in

With Prime Minister Prem who painted the dining room Elizabeth-purple.

Their Majesties appoint MF Knight Grand Cross. Looking on, U.S. Ambassador William Brown, GM's Roger Smith and Apple Computer's John Sculley.

In the Singapore stock exchange trading pit.

Kip Shanghaied.

Aboard, four "sons of . . .": Deng Pufang, son of China's boss; Christopher Forbes; Jack Ford, son of former President Gerald Ford; Mark Thatcher, son of Britain's Prime Minister Margaret Thatcher.

Who needs horsepower?

Olympic time in Seoul.

Seoulees.

Feasting amid flowers.

Tokyo's Ginza now out-Times-Squares Times Square.

the United States about various countries that are not only on the make but are making it.

Six months and thirty thousand miles after we steamed out of New York Harbor on a cold day in January, I think both sides believed we had made some progress.

So that was one kind of party.

Here's another.

The Château de Balleroy in Normandy was the first of our major overseas properties. I have rhapsodized in an earlier chapter about the stunning effect that France's greatest architect, François Mansart's seventeenth-century gem has on most first-time visitors. It has that effect on me, too, whenever I return there, which, unhappily, is very seldom—in fact, usually only once a year, the ballooning weekend.

Unlike many of its Norman neighbors, Château de Balleroy was never designed as a fortress. The moat was never filled, for example, and the windows climb from floor to ceiling because by the time Mansart took on the job nobody seemed all that worried about archers and

The Japanese don't argue back.

Returning through the Canal, July 8, 1988: between passages, some Pacific Rim accomplishments.

Grand old man of ballooning, France's late Charles Dolfus.

catapults and muskets anymore. The King's power was great enough by 1620 that strongholds in the country could no longer stand him off if the nobles had a falling out with the crown. The result, for all its impressive facade, is a building of surprising delicacy and grace. There are plenty more massive châteaux with many more rooms and a lot more land, but Balleroy is unique—a kind of great outdoor Fabergé Imperial fantasy.

Aside from being one of our favorite Forbes outposts and the site of the world's first international balloon museum—a tribute to those lighter-than-air Montgolfier brothers who masterminded the world's first balloon ascent—Balleroy has also become the venue for one of the most colorful events in the aviation world, the annual Forbes International Balloon Meet.

For the last fourteen years, on the second weekend in June, we have invited a rotating roster of premier balloonists from the countries that engage in this most beguiling of sports to come together as our guests for a three-day weekend of airborne festivities, noncompetitive camaraderie, hearty Norman fare and, of course, as many free-floating balloon ascensions as the weather and the winds will allow.

Everybody who attends is a guest of *Forbes* Magazine—we usually have between twenty and thirty "visiting" balloons and occasionally

Filling 'em up on the field and at the table.

At Balleroy, Armand Hammer with, Anne, the Queen of Romania.

The back's as striking as the front.

Microwave it isn't.

Making Mick Jagger an honorary hot aeronaut.

hot-air blimps—and each year we try to include different balloonists so that as many outstanding contributors to the sport as possible can be saluted and suitably celebrated.

To our delight, an invitation to this International Balloon Fête has come to be a hot ticket in the world of hot-air, and, *Forbes* being *Forbes*, what started out as a Normandy equivalent of our New Jersey Capitalist Tool motorcycle runs has, over the years, become a much sought-after invitation in the international corporate and diplomatic communities.

If a dinner cruise aboard the *Highlander* has become synonymous with floating friendships within the higher reaches of the business community, wafting over the French countryside in a wicker basket with, say, Rupert Murdoch, Gianni Agnelli, Walter Cronkite, or Ford CEO Don Peterson has transformed many a jaded CEO into a modern-day Jules Verne.

Balloons are like that.

What happens on a Balleroy balloon weekend?

A lot.

On Friday, the first night, the invited international balloon captains and their teams at a traditional Norman banquet are presented with awards, certificates and, usually, a specially commissioned piece of Balleroy pottery to commemorate the occasion. And, as part of the evening's ceremonies, we work to match up each visiting team with eager nonballoonist guests for a flight the next day.

Then, between the main course and dessert, the year's new fantasy balloon is dramatically unveiled. Usually it is the shaped envelope designed by Don Cameron that we have introduced on our most recent Friendship Tour. This year, for example, it was the towering reincarnation of *Suleyman the Magnificent*, the exotic tribute during our '88 Turkey tour.

Then, after dessert, and after we've confirmed our nonballooning guests for their next day's flight, we readjourn to the great lawn in back of the Château and become transformed into children again in the festive reflection of some of the best fireworks to be seen anywhere.

Everybody in the town of Balleroy has already

Mavis and Jay Leno.

ON THE SOFA IN THE GRAND SALON:

received a printed invitation to the event, so young and old, friends and neighbors, farmers and financiers—altogether maybe fifteen thousand people—turn out together for a skyful of Roman candles, star shells, laser beams, classical music and often a wondrous water display to top it all off. With Balleroy in the background, and the anticipation of the weekend's diversions that lie ahead, our guests find themselves savoring an evening that even the indefatigable Mansart himself could scarcely have imagined.

Every year we accommodate as many of our distinguished guests as possible at the Château, but, as the festival has grown in popularity, there is an inevitable spillover into neighborhood châteaux and area hotels and inns.

ET . . .

. . . and MF.

Tim Forbes and wife Anne Harrison.

Mrs. Gordon Forbes and Christopher Forbes.

Author Nick Dunne . . .

. . . comes out for air.

Former United States Information Agency Chief Charles and Mary Jane Wick.

Rob and Cam Canion of Compaq Computer Corp.

A pause for Rolling Stone's Jann and Jane Wenner.

Betsy Cronkite grins as Walter eyes the future.

Then comes Saturday morning, *early* Saturday morning, and, assuming the wind is under ten knots—five knots is just about perfect—we rally the visiting teams and start the work of getting the various Forbes shapes into the air.

Some of our balloons are year-round residents of Balleroy and are familiar spectacles at festivals, galas, charity events and civic celebrations all over Europe. *Forbes* has established a familiar and well-regarded identity with ballooning on the Continent that is quite independent of my own participation in the sport. We regard their regular appearances there as effective promotion as well as good fun.

Other shapes will have been brought over with us on the *Capitalist Tool* from their summering and wintering headquarters at home in Timberfield and will return with us at the end of the weekend.

As this magical menagerie begins to take shape—the *Golden Temple* of Japan, the *Great Sky Elephant* from the Thailand trip, the *Sphinx* that conquered Cairo, the bust of *Bee-*

Newlyweds Shirley Lord and Abe Rosenthal.

Speak no evil, hear no evil, see no evil. King Michael of Romania, his Queen Anne and Countess de Breteuil.

Mrs. Douglas MacArthur and Hubert de Givenchy.

Daughter Susan and editor-author-journalist Jim Brady.

thoven that bemused both East and West Germans, the hugest *Harley* in captivity—photographers click away to their hearts' content from vertiginous perches on the loftiest tower of the Château and from hovering helicopters.

Finally, transformed from lifeless multicolored pancakes spread out on the meadow, one by one each great bauble rises slowly into the sky, first the Forbes fleet and then the guest balloons.

Local Boy Scouts supplement the chase teams that track the balloons and help to deflate the envelopes upon landing. And each balloon carries an invitation to the Château for any farmer whose field becomes an impromptu landing site, together with a complimentary bottle of champagne.

We usually stage a Saturday noontime reception for the balloonists and our other guests. There are local trips into the countryside—and more balloon rides—during the afternoon; a grand Norman-style barbecue that evening; and then on Sunday morning, for those who are awake early enough, a special "balloon" Mass in the Château's church at which the local priest delivers his sermon from a balloon basket.

Hot air lifts hang glider.

Balloon day at Balleroy.

For a send off, French horns sound off.

The climax of what some might call a weekend of climaxes arrives in the form of an afternoon open house for the local officialdom —mayors, prefects, heads of police and fire departments—built around an all-ages open-air picnic on the grass, complete with costumed folk dancers, nonstop music courtesy of the local orchestra, free-falling parachutists and, naturally, more and still more balloon ascensions.

Nobody much wants to leave, and nobody much does until it grows too dark to distinguish perhaps the most spectacular balloon of all— the inflatable *Balleroy*, from the real château.

Then the Normandy stars come out, and we all go home—to dream about yet more balloons, and next year's celebration.

Still feel like celebrating?
Have I got a night for you.

Thousands RSVP to the traditional International Invitational Balloon Meet fireworks invitation.

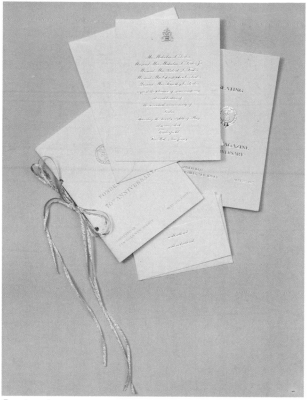

Invitations . . .

. . . and income.

70th Anniversary Issue

JULY 13, 1987   THREE DOLLARS FIFTY CENTS

Forbes

CAPITALISM
IS BY NATURE
A FORM OF CHANGE
AND NEVER IS,
NEVER CAN BE,
STATIONARY

One guest called it a combination of *Brigadoon* and *The Great Gatsby*.

Another wag referred to it as "Woodstock for Capitalists."

The papers called it "The Party of the Century."

In any event, the year was 1987 and the date was May 28. *Forbes* was celebrating its seventieth anniversary, and my children and I decided to make it as really memorable as we possibly could for our 1,100 guests (and three hundred chauffeurs, thirty-eight helicopter pilots and dozens of local policemen and firemen).

We'd had a 50th Anniversary Party for the magazine in 1967 with some eight hundred guests, also at Timberfield, but most of them had since retired or stopped going to parties altogether, so we would be entertaining a whole new generation of movers and shakers.

More than a year ahead of time I sat down with my sons and we started seriously to figure out how we could make the 70th a genuinely awesome and meaningful occasion.

Our first challenge was to put together a 70th Anniversary issue of *Forbes*, a feat that was brilliantly pulled off by the project's chief editor, Bill Baldwin. The result turned out to be the largest revenue-producing issue in *Forbes* history—$10,061,544.76.

One of the first things we did early in the year was send a personal letter from me to the key chief executives of the country—the people about whom we report, write, ride and deride —asking them to circle the date, May 28. We said that we were hoping to make it a night not to be forgotten.

Then we set out on the journey of a thousand steps to decide who would do what.

Working through Beverly Sills, we engaged John Conklin, one of the key set designers for the Metropolitan Opera, to create for us a mythical-Scottish-castle effect at Timberfield, complete with a great pavilion for cocktails and another romantic structure with the feel of a great Scottish castle's dining hall for dinner. The result was a twenty-six-foot-high dining tent that comfortably sheltered 120 tables which could conveniently be serviced by some

38 choppers and 32 chefs.

GE's Welch and NBC's Brokaw.

Fed Chairman Greenspan ponders
Barbara Walters.

two-hundred and seventy captains and waiters.

But how would people know that it was Scotland without a wee bit of the gloaming, and what good was gloaming without a piper or two?

I won't belabor the details, but will only say that we ultimately engaged 121 pipers and drummers, that John Conklin created some of the finest gloaming this side of Aberdeenshire, and that the artificial mist that was laid down as the pipers made their eerily appropriate entrance down the wooded hillside would have softened even the heart of an Englishman.

Genius maestro Sean Driscoll of caterers Glorious Foods, plied us with an incredible array of test meals, and the outcome was, well, incredible:

Thirty-two chefs would ply their skills to 1,600 pounds of Scotch salmon, 24 hams, 700 baby pheasants, 120 pounds of foie gras, 450 pounds of haricots verts, 24 legs of lamb, 60 country pâtés, 3,000 artichokes, 500 pints of raspberries and strawberries, 150 quarts of ice cream and 15 gallons of butterscotch sauce.

For dessert, they had another wonderful idea. Why not grace each table with a cake decorated with a replica, in frosting, of the first cover of *Forbes*, published September 15, 1917, and top off the lot with a special batch of "capitalist cookies"?

The logistics turned out to be even more daunting than we had imagined: parking for several hundred cars, a traffic controller for the helicopters, a special menu and feeding facilities for the pilots, the chauffeurs and the more than six hundred staff workers it took to orchestrate the evening.

That was just for starters.

The celebrated Grucci family of fireworks fame happily agreed to plan and detonate the special effects, and Lester Lanin said he'd be

Ann Getty, Jerry Zipkin, and Miki Sarofim.

Carl and Liba Icahn.

Alison and Leonard Stern with Patricia Kluge.

delighted to set the musical pace for after-dinner dancing. President Reagan, sadly, had to send his regrets as keynote speaker, but then White House Chief of Staff Howard Baker, New Jersey Governor Thomas Kean and Senator Bill Bradley all volunteered their services and performed nobly and wittily as a trio of MCs.

The guest list, with its multiple possibilities for receiving-line gaffes and seating catastrophes, was handled with unflappable insouciance by my unflappably insouciant son Kip, who somehow also managed to have the engraved Tiffany bowls—souvenirs of the evening —at all the proper places, with the correct personal anniversary or birthday date for the right recipients.

A year's worth of planning, countless meetings, last-minute crises, late acceptances, cancellations, a deranged drawbridge, a suit of armor with arms that threatened to become permanently paralytic—we lived through them all.

Our illustrious guests, especially the wives who are called on for corporate entertaining (all Chiefs and no Indians) could understand the vastness of the undertaking.

I believe it was the architect Mies Van Der Rohe who observed that "God is in the details." He was speaking architecturally, but he could just as aptly have been describing our experi-

ence with the 70th. What our guests saw that night was what they got. What they didn't see —and shouldn't have seen—was what it took to create the illusion of all that gracious inevitability.

The party was on a Thursday. The following Sunday we gave a scaled-down repeat for our local motorcycle club, the Capitalist Tools. The original was absolutely the biggest party I've ever thrown. Originally, I had thought we would wait until the 75th, but I'm glad we didn't. This way we don't have to wait too long until the next one.

What thoughts surface as I reminisce about that magical eve?

For one thing, it set me thinking about why we entertain the way we do.

MUSIC'S MAGIC:

Anna and Rupert Murdoch.

Ivana and Donald Trump.

Howard Baker and Henry K.

Betts and Wallace Forbes with hit-songwriting daughter Alex (center), and son Bruce with friend.

Mrs. Ahmet Ertegun, Irving Lazar and Reinaldo Herrera.

The ideal guest, from our point of view, is a cordial and happy couple whose company is also a major advertiser. But it's not that simple. Many of these people become our friends, yet sometimes part of our job is to be editorially critical of their on-the-job performance *between* parties. Obviously, this can sometimes put a unique kind of strain on our role as host, theirs as guests.

But the basics remain. Our experience has shown that just about everybody feels at ease when they know that you're happy to see them, say so, and show it. Also, that most people like to meet other people outside their day-to-day routine. We've found that show-business glitterati are intrigued to meet business types. And, even more so, vice versa.

I'm reminded of Thoreau's observation about his own approach to entertaining. Not chiefly known for his lavish revels on the Concord

Bill Paley and Brooke Astor.

David and Peggy Rockefeller.

Aileen Mehle ("Suzy") and Jerry Hall.

Sir James Goldsmith and daughter Alex.

Irena and Lane Kirkland.

From out of the hills 100 pipers, 20 drummers and 1 pipe major.

Claudia and Gordon Forbes.

Granddaughters Catherine and Moira cutting a caper.

party circuit, I think, that he was onto something, as usual. "I have three chairs in my house," he recalls in *Visitors*; "one for solitude, two for friendship, and three for society."

As for my chair number one, I'm sitting on that one right now. If I had to pick one single thing that would be on top, it's being at this desk. I was here this morning at six-thirty, and I'll probably be here at six tonight as well. It's fun to be at the wheel when you're the boss.

As for my chair number two, I'm going to substitute the Greek word *agape* for Thoreau's

concept of friendship—love for family: Steve, Bob, Kip, Tim, Moira; for my nine grandchildren; for Roberta, Wally, Duncan, Bruce and Gordon; for my mother, Adelaide Stevenson, unawaredly the first feminist Keynesian; and, of course, for father B.C., my Scottish tap root.

Had my father been there at the head table that midsummer's eve, I feel confident of three things: that he would have been wearing his kilt, been appalled at the expense, and been secretly pleased, in his own way, that we could afford it.

TEMPUS FUGIT
so catch it if you can.

From The Sayings of Chairman Malcolm

Grateful acknowledgment is made to the following for the use of their photos and illustrations which appear on the following pages:

PHOTO CREDITS

Acken, Paul—232/top. 234/bottom L., 236/bottom.
Alexaki, Nicholas—33/R.
AMF, Inc.—107.
Anderson, Bob and Ed Jafee—32/bottom.
Archive of Agusta Aerospace Corporation—123/bottom.
Ardiles-Arce, Jaime—171/all, 172/all, 173/all.
Atelier von Behr—14/center L., 30/R., 31/all.
Attaway, Roy—48/3rd R., 62–63/spread, 63/top.
Bahuchet, Gerard—145.
Barlow, Peter—48/top L.
Barrow, Julian—18/bottom R.
Buckley, Christopher—80/top L., 82, 83/bottom, 84, 87/all,
　89/top L., 92, 93.
Byron—174.
Carmine—15/bottom middle, bottom R., 17/top R., center R.
Chiasson, John (Gamma-Liaison)—224–225, 249/top L., bottom L.,
　252/bottom, 253/R.
Christie's London—212/top L.
Crossley, T & D—37.
Curran, H. Peter—54/center L. & R., bottom, 219, 220/bottom, 223/
　bottom.
Davis, Glen A.—endpapers, 19/bottom L. & R., 20–21, 44/all, 45/all,
　46/all, 47/all, 77/top & center R., 99, 100/bottom, 101/bottom, 105,
　108/all, 111/top L., bottom L. & R., 113/inset, 114/center, 115/
　bottom, 116, 117/bottom, 118/bottom L., 122/top R., center R. &
　bottom R., 123/top, 130/all, 131/all, 133/bottom L. & R., 153/all,
　154, 155, 156, 157/all, 158/top, 159, 161/bottom L. & bottom R.,
　162/bottom, 163/top R., 165/center, 166, 167/top & bottom, 168–
　169, 184/all, 185/all, 186/bottom L. & bottom R., 187/all, 188/all,
　188-189/spread, 191/bottom L. & R., 192/top, 196/bottom, 202/
　center L., 229/top R., bottom R., 230/all, 231/all, 232/bottom, 233/
　center L & R., 235/all, 236/center L., 246/top L.
Dee, D. James—22, 26/medal inset, 28/bottom, 134/top, 150, 160,
　170, 248/all.
Delar—30/L.
Dennis, Lisl—68/top & center, 69/bottom.
Dixson, Chuck—77/bottom, 238/all.
Ehrenclou, John—52/R., 55/top R.
Elder, Jim—16/top L., 18/bottom L., 190/top.
Endress, John Paul—96–97, 100–101/spread.
Engzelius, Dr. Jan—114/top, 117/top.
Fein, Nat—34/top.
Fergusson, Wm.—23/top.
Forbes, Christopher—76/top L., 233/bottom.
Forbes, Malcolm—15/center R.
Forbes, Robert L.—50, 52/L., 53/all, 54/top L., 55/top L., center L. &
　R., 70/L., 73/top R., 124, 126/top L., 134/center & bottom R., 135/
　all, 138/all, 139/top, 143/bottom, 144, 147/all, 151, 158/bottom,
　161/top, 163/bottom L., 164, 167/center, 176/top L., 202/bottom
　R., 214/2nd L., 233/top, 240/top R., 241/top, 247/bottom R.
Forbes, Timothy C.—133/top.
Foto Looman—60.
Gelb, Ross—121/top.
Goddard, Martyn—165/top.
Guillou, Alain—118/top & center L., 118–119/spread, 125/top R.,
　126/top R., 128–129, 132, 137, 139/bottom, 140, 142, 143/top,
　148, 149, 182/top L., 182-183/spread, 194/top, 196/top, 197/center
　L., 199/top, 202/center R., 240/bottom R., 241/bottom R., 247/L.
Haas, Lt. John—236/top L.
Henry, Diana—19/top R.
Hilliard, Mary—19/center.
Ienatsch, Nick—114/bottom, 115/top.

Jenkins, Kevin—239/all.
Joel, Yale—17/bottom L.
Johnsrud, A. L.—34/bottom.
Knudsen, R. L., (PHC, USN)—48/2nd L.
Koch, John—15/center middle, 16/center L.
Korb, Stephane—220/top.
Kupjack, Jay—213.
Kusumoto, Sam—227/all, 228/all.
Lal, Nitin—201/bottom L., 202/top L.
Library of Congress—211/inset photo.
Luce's Studio—24/bottom.
Makos, Christopher—242, 243/all, 244/all, 245/all.
Manarchy, Dennis—title page.
Marcus, Helen—74/bottom.
May, Clifford D.—125/bottom R.
Mays, Steven—221/bottom.
McNally, Joe—66–67.
Milet, Jacques—48–49, 55/bottom L.
Moskowitz, Sonia—250/bottom R., 253/bottom L.
Mumma, Moira—191/top.
Nationaal Foto—69/top.
Nelson, Otto E.—120, 193, 208/center R., 214/top L., 214/bottom R.,
　216/all, 217/center, 218/all.
Nichols, Mary E.—192/center R., 194/bottom, 195, 197/top L. & top
　R., bottom R., 198, 200, 201/top, 201/center R., 202/bottom L.,
　203.
Outlaw Biker magazine—111/top middle & top R.
Özözlu, Halûk—165/bottom.
Pfotenhauer, Alexander F.—17/center L., bottom middle, bottom R.,
　18/top L., top R., center, 19/top L., 48/3rd L. & 4th L., 64–65, 70/
　R., 71, 73/center R., bottom L. & R., 74/top L. & R.
Pfotenhauer, Ingo—48/bottom L.
Phillips, Robert—76/top R., 79, 80/center L., 80–81/spread, 83/top,
　85/all, 86, 89/top R., center L. & R., bottom R., 90, 91/all, 94–95.
Purpura & Kisner Inc.—182/center L., bottom L., 186/top, center R.
Qwarnström, Anders—240/center R., 246/bottom R.
Röhrscheid, Jürgen—127.
Roosevelt, The Hon. Selwa—234/top L. & R., 237/all.
Schulenburg, Fritz von der—178/all, 179/all.
Scott, Rey—58–59.
Sherman, Pierre—249/top R., bottom R., 250/top L. & R., 251/all,
　252/top L. & R., all center, 253/top L.
Slack, Hank—236/center R.
Stahl, Bill (*Daily News*)—106.
Stein, Larry—29/3rd R. & bottom R., 51, 175, 176/bottom R., 176–
　177/spread, 181/top L., 204, 205, 206, 207/all, 208/top L. & R.,
　bottom L., 209/all, 210/all, 211/all documents, 212/top R., center,
　bottom R., 214/center R., 215, 217/top, 221/top, 222/all, 223/top.
Thomas, Kirk S.—241/bottom L.
Tucker, Steven—176/bottom L.
Walz, Barbra—103/all, 109/all.
Wynn, Dan—17/center middle, 177/bottom R.
Young, Jerry—125/bottom L.

ILLUSTRATIONS

Farrow, Tim—226.
Green, Peter—217/bottom.
Kubinyi, Laslo—78, 152.
Mansfield, Robert—136, 162/top.
Marcus, Ed—40/all, 41/all.
Müller, Kees—68/bottom.

All materials not otherwise acknowledged have been provided by the Forbes Archives. Special thanks to Image Photographic Laboratory, K + L Custom PhotoGraphics, and Motal Custom Darkrooms for their darkroom and copy expertise.